P9-BYB-835

Linda Page

N.D., Ph.D

Sexuality

Enhancing
Your Body Chemistry

The Healthy Healing Library Series

Copyright 1998
by
Linda Rector Page
All Rights Reserved

No part of this book may be
copied or reproduced
in any form without
the written consent
of the publisher.

ISBN:1-884334-15-6
Published by Healthy Healing
Publications, Inc.
P.O. 436, Carmel Valley, CA 93924

Please note: The products recommended by Dr. Page in this book are chosen by a completely objective product review process. The products are for your information only, and are not intended as medical advice. Dr. Page is in no way compensated by any company for her recommendations.

About the Author....

L inda Page has been working in the fields of nutrition and herbal medicine both professionally and as a personal lifestyle choice, since the early seventies. She is a certified Doctor of Naturopathy and Ph.D., with extensive experience in formulating herbal combinations. She received a Doctorate of Naturopathy from the Clayton College of Natural Health in 1988, and a Ph.D. in Nutritional Therapy from the American Holistic College of Nutrition in 1989. She is a member of both the American and California Naturopathic Medical Associations.

Linda opened and operated the "Rainbow Kitchen," a natural foods restaurant, then became a working partner in The Country Store Natural Foods store. Linda is also the founder and formulator of Crystal Star Herbal Nutrition, a manufacturer of over 250 premier herbal compounds. A major, cutting edge influence in the herbal medicine field, Crystal Star Herbal Nutrition products are carried by over twenty-five hundred natural food stores in the U.S. and around the world.

Linda has written four successful books and a Library Series of specialty books in the field of natural healing. Today, she is the editor-in-chief of a national monthly, natural health newsletter, The Natural Healing Report. She has a weekly CBS News TV segment where she discusses a wide range of natural healing topics, and she has her own weekly, one-hour radio talk show program called "The World of Healthy Healing." Linda also lectures around the country, contributes articles to national publications, is regularly featured on radio and television, and is an adjunct professor at Clayton College of Natural Health.

Continuous research in all aspects of the alternative healing world has been the cornerstone of success for her reference work Healthy Healing now in its tenth edition, with sales of almost a million books.

Cooking For Healthy Healing, now in its second revised edition, is a companion to Healthy Healing. It draws on both the recipes from the Rainbow Kitchen and the more defined, lifestyle diets that she has developed for healing. This book contains thirty-three diet programs, and over 900 healthy recipes.

In How To be Your Own Herbal Pharmacist, Linda addresses the rising appeal of herbs and herbal healing in America. This book is designed for those wishing to take more definitive responsibility for their health through individually developed herbal combinations.

Another popular work is Linda's party reference book, Party Lights, written with restaurateur and chef Doug Vanderberg. Party Lights, takes healthy cooking one step further by adding fun to a good diet.

Published by Healthy Healing Publications, 1998

Bibliography

Jensen, Dr. Bernard. *Love, Sex & Nutrition.* 1988

Walker, Dr. Morton. *Sexual Nutrition.* 1994

Page, Linda R. *Healthy Healing* - Tenth Edition. 1997

Page, Linda R., N.D. Ph.D. *Renewing Female Balance.* 1997

Peiper, Dr. Howard & Nina Anderson, *Crystalloid Electrolytes,* 1997

Tunella, Kim, C.D.C. "6-Week Program For Diet and Lifestyle Changes". 1995

Stansbury, Jll E., N.D. "Fortifying Fertility With Vitamins And Herbs", *Nutrition Science News.* Dec. 1997

Hurley, Judith B. "A Women's Medicine Chest". *Vegetarian Times.* July 1996

Herbal Research Pub. *The Protocol Journal Of Botanical Medicine,* 1995

Orey, Cal. "Ten Healthy Tips To Help You Feel Sexier", *Let's Live.* November 1996

Laskow, Leonard, M. D. *Healing With Love.* 1992

Murray, Michael T., N.D. *Encyclopedia of Nutritional Supplements.* 1996

Brown, Royden. *How To Live The Millennium - Bee Pollen Bible.* 1989

O'Neill, Hugh. "Love Is The Drug". *Men's Health.* November 1997

Murray, Michael, N.D. "Sexual Vitality for Men & Women", *Let's Live.* May 1994

Orey, Cal. "Spice Up Your Life With Erotic Edibles", *Lets Live.* February 1995

Gladstar, Rosemary. *Herbal Healing For Women.* 1993

Bertani, Elizabeth, "A Is For Aphrodisiacs", *Natural Foods Merchandiser.* December 1996

Valnet, Jean, M.D. *The Practice of Aromatherapy.* 1990

Whitaker, Julian, M.D. *Breath-Taking Sex.* 1994

Books In The Library Series

Dr. Page's written papers are thoroughly researched - through empirical observation as well as from documented evidence. Studies are ongoing and updated at Healthy Healing Publications, P.O. Box 436, Carmel Valley, CA 93924.

As affordable, high quality health care ir America becomes more difficult to finance anc obtain, natural therapies and persona wellness techniques are receiving more at tention and favor. Over 75% of American: now use some form of natural health care from vitamins, to cleansing diets, to guidec imagery, to herbal supplements.

Everyone needs more information about these methods to make informed choices for their own health and that of their families The Healthy Healing Library Series was created to answer this neec - with inexpensive, up-to-date books on the subjects people wani to hear about the most.

The lifestyle therapy programs discussed in each book has beer developed over the last fifteen years from the reported response: and successful healing results experienced by literally thousand: of people. In addition, the full time research team at Healthy Heal ing Publications, Inc. investigates herbs, herbal combinations anc herbal therapies from around the world for their availability anc efficacy. You can feel every confidence that the recommendations are synthesized from real people with real problems who got rea results.

Herbal medicines are highlighted in these books because they are in the forefront of modern science today. Herbal healing has the proven value of ancient wisdom and a safety record of centu- ries. Yet, science can only quantify, isolate, and assay to under- stand. Herbs respond to these methods, but they are so much more than the sum of their parts. God shows his face a little in herbs. They, too, have an ineffable quality.

Fortunately for us, our bodies know how to use herbs without our brains having to know why.

Table of Contents

Sexuality
Enhancing Your Body Chemistry

Love is the most powerful energy in the world. It is so powerful that it can transform a person totally - from the inside out. More than that, love is so powerfully dynamic that it can change the world around a loving person, and from there to the spheres of countless others.
The impact of a loving heart has no limits.

Love pulls us with a magnetic force toward unity and wholeness. When a relationship blossoms into love, the sexual act of giving and receiving erotic physical pleasure, emotional nourishment and spiritual oneness with our loved one becomes a fundamental human expression. Sexual fulfillment can provide ultimate joy in shared intimacy, orgasm, and love. Loving sex can bring with it a supreme source of mutual healing and awakening of the spirit. Sexual closeness generates a potent healing energy, restorative and nurturing for each partner.

But great sex depends on more than just falling in love - even with the right person - it also depends upon good health. Most of our sexuality problems come from a poor diet and life-style burnout. Even if sexual problems are psychological, nutrition and sex are still intimately related because psychological sex problems can be rooted in chemical or glandular imbalances.

Is sexual chemistry real? We tend to think that our modern era is the only one beset with libido-lowering elements. Certainly there is no question that our nutrient-poor, high-fat diets, over-use of drugs and stimulants, and high-pressure lifestyles lead to low energy and lack of time for love.

But the reality is that humanity in every era has felt the need for help in the sexual and reproductive area. After all, this part of our lives is at the most elemental center of our being.

The complex process of sexual function begins in the brain. Sexual response for us is not instinctive, as it is in animals. It is purposeful. The *"sexual chemistry"* we experience with another human being is **brain chemistry** rather than **body chemistry**, even though it follows through to body responses.

The brain initiates sexual feelings through the hypothalamus which acts as a switchboard for incoming nerve and sensory impulses, like smell, sound and touch. A chemical released by the hypothalamus triggers the pituitary gland to release gland-stimulating hormones, and also directly stimulates the brain to produce sexual arousal. And it can all happen in an instant.... sometimes at first sight!

The first sensations of sexual energy and urgency **we** notice come from the glands which produce sex hormones. The reason we are so deeply affected by sex is that every gland plays a part in the release and function of sexual response.

While men and women respond differently to the chemical stimulation from the brain, sensitivity for both sexes stems from the sex center in the hypothalamus gland. The hypothalamus uses its nerve links to the endocrine system for direct and indirect exchanges between the brain and the glands. Body imbalances from stress, fatigue, or a poor diet adversely affect the way the hypothalamus functions.

What makes us sexually aroused?

Most of the time, all five senses take part in sexual arousal. First, we may see someone that stirs a visual attractive response within us. Then, visual "excitement" may be enhanced by an attractive voice or words. Smell is incredibly important to erotic attraction, whether it is the fragrance of an essential oil or the person's own natural body aroma. Touch, the most arousing

of the senses, can ignite tingling from a mere brushing of hands. Touch joins taste in the sweetness of a kiss.

Our senses spark our emotions, then our stimulated glands send out their hormones, then the nervous system engages pelvic nerves where tissues begin to swell with blood. Adrenaline is released from the adrenal glands, our hearts beat faster, our breathing increases and so does oxygen uptake; our sex glands begin to secrete lubricating fluids. As the levels of pleasure rise, the brain's limbic system electrifies, releasing pleasure-producing chemicals, sweeping into powerful vibratory intensity for orgasm. It's no wonder that these powerful body processes need to be in good health to function well in sexual activity.

Our glands are such a key part of the sexual response. In fact, sexual arousal depends on healthy internal signaling between brain, senses, nerves, glands, blood vessels and sex gonads. Sexual delight and satisfaction need balanced, working glands to produce the necessary sex hormones.

There are two types of glands: 1) Exocrine glands regulated by the hypothalamus, secrete their fluids through ducts, like the salivary and mammary glands. **2) Endocrine glands** secrete **hormones** directly into the bloodstream - especially those related to sex function.

How do the glands work during sex?

* The pituitary gland governs the thyroid and the hormone-releasing sex glands.

* The pineal, hypothalamus and pituitary glands stimulate the brain.

* The thyroid and parathyroid stimulate the sex organs.

* The adrenal glands boost energy levels for sexual activity, (Pay attention to your adrenal health on a regular basis, because weak adrenals reduce the desire for sex and increase sensitivity to stress.)

* The ovaries produce female sex hormones and regulate female cycles.

* The testes produce male sex hormones and are the site of sperm production.

* The prostate gland produces fluid to protect the sperm.

Hormones are the other key to sexual response.

There are three hormone types:

1) Polypeptide hormones, the messengers that trigger the release of sex hormones like estrogen, testosterone and progesterone and also act as neurotransmitters in the brain.

2) Steroid hormones, like the sex hormones estrogen, testosterone, and progesterone.

3) Prostaglandins, that stimulate the production of steroid hormones, affect blood pressure and possibly the body's "electrical" response.

Is there any way to determine and analyze your gland and hormone health profile?

Here's a resource: The **Los Gatos Longevity Institute** (Los Gatos, CA. 408-358-8855. www.AntiAging.com) uses leading edge medical technology and alternative medicine with state-of-the-art testing equipment that can determine your bio-markers. Blood levels, body composition, your diet, exercise habits, emotional patterns and stress factors are brought into the health modeling picture. Rejuvenation programs include nutritional medicine, natural hormone replacement, menopausal and andropausal therapy, complex cholesterol and stress management programs. All anti-aging issues are addressed, including stopping the progression of age related degenerative diseases, and slowing the rate at which your body ages, revitalizing your energy level, libido, and sexual performance.

But sexuality goes even deeper than hormones, because at their most elemental level hormonal reactions are due to the stimulation and activation of certain enzymes. Amazingly enough, human sexuality really is determined largely by what we eat. **Nutrients can stoke the fires of passion and sexuality because that's where we get the gland and hormone-stimulating enzymes.**

The best enzymes are contained in fresh vegetables, fresh fruits, and vegetable and fruit juices, sprouts, sea vegetables, whole grains, nuts, seeds and beans, cultured foods, and fresh fish and sea foods. Enzymes are much more heat-sensitive than vitamins and are the first to be destroyed during cooking, pasteurization, canning, micro-waving, or fast food processing, or anything that heats your food above 118 degrees Fahrenheit.

* I often recommend a good food enzyme supplement. Two of my favorites are REZYME by Nature's Secret and ADVANCED ENZYME SYSTEM by Rainbow Light.

If you microwave your food most of the time, you're not doing your love life any good. The enzyme supply in your food is dramatically affected by the use of a microwave because it destroys them. Enzymes are also destroyed by substances like tobacco, alcohol, caffeine, fluorides, chlorine in drinking water, air pollution, chemical additives and many medicines. Enzymes are extremely sensitive to heat. Even low degrees of heat can incapacitate food enzymes and greatly reduce assimilation ability. Heat above 120° F. completely destroys them. Eating fresh foods not only requires much less digestive work from the body, but fresh foods can provide more of their own enzymes to work with yours.

Eliminate the junk from your life for more sexuality.
That includes junk foods. A diet of chemicalized foods (even if you're a teen with raging hormones) is **a major contributing factor** to a lack of sexual desire and sexual performance.

If your body is clogged with chemical food additives, meats and dairy foods from hormone-injected animals and pesticides from sprayed produce, you'll seldom feel like making love even when everything else in life is going well. A pollutant-free body can feel things deeper, better and longer.... really.

Watch out for these three libido repressors:

1) Drugs of all kinds affect sexuality. ▪ Tranquilizers immediately impair sexual function. ▪ Cocaine, heroin and marijuana, regardless of their short-term mood altering properties, result in loss of sexual interest over the long term. ▪ Nicotine impairs circulation to the pelvic area, contributes to impotence, and may interfere with a woman's orgasm. ▪ Alcohol destroys testosterone, the male sex hormone.

2) Sugar initially stimulates a kind of short term energy, but then drops your energy below its previous level, sometimes contributing to mild depression. Sugar also lowers endorphins, chemicals that promote your sense of pleasure.

3) Fatty, fried foods contribute to clogging your arteries, reducing blood flow and oxygen to the brain where sexual arousal starts. Reduced sexual interest, sensory nerve response and performance ability can result.

The Transformative Power of a Nutritious Diet:

No matter what sexuality problem you may be addressing, a healthy diet rich in nutrients is the center piece of a vibrant and healthy sex life. Research shows that certain nutrients help awaken libido, boost sexual vigor and stamina, and heighten sexual excitement for both partners.

For example, the brain, nerves and glands are strengthened by foods high in phosphatides, silicon, fatty acids and zinc. Some nutrients can even help combat sexual disorders like impotence, difficulty achieving orgasm, menstrual and menopausal complaints, prostate problems and herpes.

What's the best diet for a healthy libido?

I believe that for any health goal you should think green and make fresh fruits and vegetables the basis of your diet. Plants have the widest array of nutrients and are the easiest for your body to use. **Green leafy vegetables** contain almost 20 times more essential nutrients, ounce for ounce, than other foods. Plants also offer the most enzymes, your body's essential link to stamina, weight control and energy - *including sexual energy!*

Further, the nutrients in deep green leafy vegetables are so important that they actually make the nutritives in other foods work more effectively. When we *don't* eat daily green vegetables, dozens of valuable cleansing, building and eliminative functions fail to work properly. **So, have a green salad every day.** And eat organically grown foods whenever possible to insure higher nutrient content and avoid toxic sprays.

Green foods also contain **chlorophyll,** the "blood" of plants, a critical nutrient that I believe is the most potent healer on our planet. Without chlorophyll, our earth would not exist as we know it today. All life on earth, so dependent on plants, would also cease to exist.

Chlorophyll has a structure almost identical to human plasma, so you're virtually giving yourself a little body balancing transfusion every time you eat it. Chlorophyll helps chelate any heavy metals, neutralizes pollutants and alkalizes any excess acidity in your body.

Okay, so veggies are sexy. What other foods nourish sexuality?

Beans, like black and kidney beans, and **whole grains** like barley and rice, nourish the kidneys and thus sexual energy. **Oysters** are rich in zinc, an important component of seminal and vaginal fluid. **Seeds** like pumpkin and sunflower are also zinc-rich; indeed most nuts and seeds keep our glands happy, our nerves calm, and our brains active.

Sea vegetables because of their high mineral (especially iodine) content, can nourish an underactive thyroid to trigger increased libido. An underactive thyroid can cause low libido. The amount of thyroid hormone released into the bloodstream determines your body's basic energy level and also affects the rate at which sex hormones are made.

Sea vegetables are delicious. Some are salty, like kelp and bladderwrack, some are sweet, like wakame, kombu and sea palm, some are tangy, like nori, arame and hijiki. Crush or snip them into soups and sauces, or use them as toppings on salads, casseroles and over pizzas. If you add sea vegetables, no other salt is needed, an advantage for a low salt diet and high blood pressure (definitely a sexuality inhibitor).

Sea vegetables by Mendocino Sea Vegetable Co. and Maine Coast Sea Vegetables are high quality products that I like.

Sprouts from seeds, grains and beans are some of the healthiest foods you can eat with living nutrients that go directly to your cells. They are good sources of protein and essential fatty acids. They are rich in enzymes, B-complex vitamins and vitamin C. They are building, warming and high in fiber and minerals with significant amounts of calcium, iron, and zinc. When a sprout mix was added to the diets of low libido animals in the San Diego Zoo, the once lethargic creatures were revitalized so much that many of them produced offspring after showing no interest in mating for several years!

Are there really any aphrodisiac foods? Certain fruits and vegetables have been associated through the ages with increased sexual strength and virility. Today nutritionists are confirming that many foods do indeed have vital nutrients that can help your love life. Some of them may surprise you.

▪ **Asparagus** contains aspartic acid (an amino acid) that neutralizes excess ammonia in the body which causes fatigue

and sexual lassitude. Asparagus also contains the alkaloid asparagine, an essential nutrient for prostate gland health.

- **Avocados** are high in potassium, magnesium, and other nutrients which supply the energy and desire for sex.

- **Carrots** have an estrogen-like compound that is said to stimulate the sexual appetite.

- **Garlic,** with compounds related to sex hormones, has been used as an aphrodisiac since Egyptian times.

- **Shiitake mushrooms** have a positive effect on sexual strength in men and a stimulating effect on women.

- **Fava beans** are rich in L-dopa, an amino acid that increases dopamine levels. Dopamine is intimately associated with sex drive in men. Fava beans have high concentrations of L-dopa; one 16-oz. can offers almost a prescription dose!

- Foods that enhance male sexuality include **zinc-rich liver, oysters, nuts, seeds and legumes.** Low zinc levels in the body result in poor sperm production and reduced testosterone levels in men. Other foods high in zinc are seafood, root vegetables, organ meats, and whole grains.

A Human Sexuality Study in San Francisco seems to validate the traditional adage about **"sowing wild oats."** It found that green-oat extract increased both sexual desire and performance in men.

Other nutrients for male sexuality include essential fatty acid like those in evening primrose oil, and vitamins. A, B$_6$, and E.

- Foods that enhance female sexuality include fennel, celery, parsley, high-lignan flaxseed oil, and seeds. The newest studies indicate that zinc-rich foods also increase sexual function in women. Synthetic estrogens like those in oral contraceptives, estrogen replacement therapy and some diuretics deplete zinc. Plant estrogens, like those in some herbs and in soy foods produce a mild, natural, beneficial estrogen effect.

▪ Studies on postmenopausal women show supplemental daily boron results in elevated estrogen levels that are the same as the levels found in women on estrogen replacement therapy. Low estrogen levels cause atrophic vaginitis, a condition that makes intercourse painful. Green leafy veggies, fruits (except citrus), nuts and legumes all have boron. If you take a boron supplement, be careful; too much boron can increase the risk of osteoporosis. About 3mg is a good daily dose.

▪ Foods with vitamin E like soy foods, wheat germ, seeds, nuts and vegetable oils are helpful for both male and female sexual problems. Studies show that some animals can't reproduce and the males' testicles shrink without vitamin E in their diet. Naturopathic doctors have used vitamin E for years to reduce vaginal dryness and increase post-menopausal libido.

Foods rich in vitamin E are also antioxidants that help protect your sex glands and hormones from free radical damage.

Fat isn't sexy:

▪ **A high fat diet decreases sexuality.** Lynn Fischer, author of *The Better Sex Diet*, says that a man eating a high-fat meal will have an immediate 25% drop in his testosterone; a women eating a high-fat meal will tend to feel sleepy.

▪ **Lower your cholesterol to raise your libido.** German and Boston University studies show that high levels of LDL cholesterol reduce the penis' ability to receive "erection signals" from the brain. When the arteries are clogged due to a high-fat diet, penis tissue flexibility is reduced which results in the shortening and weakening of erections.

But there's more to the story of fats and libido. There's no question that **unhealthy, saturated fats** from meats, dairy and fried foods decrease testosterone, increase abnormal sperm, correlate with low birth weight babies, and lower human breast milk quality. But many Americans have gone the "all or nothing" route to a no-fat diet, and that means they lose out on the **healthy fats** needed for healthy sexuality. *Unsaturated fats,* like those found in olive, flax and canola oils provide **essential fatty acids** the body needs to protect cell membranes and form the prostaglandins (tissue-like hormones) that control gland functions like those important for slimness, easy menstrual periods and sperm production.

Here's what essential fatty acids can do for your sexuality:
  * Essential fatty acids (EFA's) help provide moisture and softness to the skin, vagina, and bladder (especially important when estrogen levels decrease).

  * EFA's help the body store fat-soluble vitamins A, D, E and K, necessary for sexual functioning.

  * EFA's supply nearly half of the calories burned by the body for energy. The gonads in particular make use of fatty acids, for hormone production and for the transfer of neurogenital impulse waves to the brain.

  * Low EFA's cause some women to experience cramping; some men experience insufficient ejaculate during intercourse. Both sexes may become infertile.

  * EFA's increase energy levels, especially physical activity. You get tired less quickly, recover faster, feel more like being sexually active and stay alert later into the evening.

So trade out the bad fats for good fats.

* Get **Alpha Linolenic acid (Omega-3 group)** from fish like trout, salmon and tuna, from raw or dry roasted nuts and seeds like flax, pumpkin, walnuts, from wheat germ and evening primrose, from dark leafy greens like kale and collards, and from sea vegetables and blue-green algae.

* Get **Linolenic acid (Omega-6 group)** from organ meats and lean turkey, from seed oils like flax, borage and sesame, legumes like soy and fava beans, leafy greens, sea vegetables and blue-green algae.

Good EFA products to consider include *ORGANIC HIGH LIGNAN FLAX OIL and *ORGANIC ESSENTIAL MAX EFA OIL by Spectrum Essentials; *ESSENTIAL WOMAN and FLAX OIL capsules by Barlean Organic Oils; *ULTIMATE OIL by Nature's Secret; and *EVENING PRIMROSE oil by Crystal Star Herbs.

Two of the superfoods are full of essential fatty acids and it's one of the reasons they have an aphrodisiac reputation - **bee pollen and royal jelly.** Both substances are also high in steroid hormonal elements similar to those secreted by the pituitary.

Bee Pollen, called the only nutritionally complete food known to man, has a long history as a sexual system vitalizer. Its many nutrients include lecithin, needed by the brain, nerves, and sexual system, and natural plant steroids thought to nourish and stimulate the glands that produce our sex hormones. The plant hormones are quite similar to the gonadotropic hormones secreted by the human pituitary to stimulate human reproductive glands. Bee Pollen is wonderful for your sex life!

Royal Jelly also contains hormone-like substances that support the glands and reproductive system, and is the only natural source of pure acetylcholine, the most important compound involved in the conduction of nerve (and sexual) impulses. In a recent study where 20mg of royal jelly daily was given to sterile male patients, sperm count and motility increased as did frequency of ejaculation also increased.

Bee pollen products to consider include BEE COMPLETE by Futurebiotics, BEE POLLEN by Y.S. Royal Jelly & Honey Farms, and BEE POLLEN by Beehive Botanicals. Royal Jelly products include ORGANIC ROYAL JELLY & SIBERIAN GINSENG by Y.S. Royal Jelly & Honey Farms, ROYAL JELLY & HONEY by PREMIER I Labs. and FRESH ROYAL JELLY by Beehive Botanicals

Should you take vitamins for better sex?

Micro-nutrients, like vitamins and minerals can shore up body nutrient deficiencies that may be affecting your sex life.

Here are special vitamins that aid in sexual vitality:

Vitamin A, an antioxidant, supports healthy adrenal function which is important for sperm production and healthy mucous membrane tissue, like that of the vagina. A deficiency causes atrophy in sex organs in rats and can impair production of sex hormones. Foods rich in vitamin A are fish, fish-liver oils, liver, eggs, cheese and yogurt.

Vitamin B$_3$ can increase blood flow to the extremities. 100mg niacin, taken about 30 minutes before sex, may enhance sexual flush, mucous membrane tingling and the intensity of the orgasm. Foods rich in B$_3$ are chicken, fish, asparagus, dates, almonds, bran, wheat germ, rice, broccoli, yogurt, seeds and nuts.

Vitamin B$_6$, is involved in making neurotransmitters like epinephrine, thought to be involved in orgasm. B$_6$ also supports adrenal function, and may help male sex drive and impotence. Foods rich in B$_6$ are wheat germ and bran, rice, whole grains, organ meats, nuts, seeds, eggs, honey and molasses.

Vitamin B$_{12}$, found in healthy sperm, may help impotence, and supports adrenal function. Foods rich in B$_{12}$ are seaweed, yogurt, milk, cheese, eggs, poultry, fish, and organ meats.

Folic Acid, an increasingly important supplement for pregnant women in preventing neural tube defects in fetuses, is also helpful for ovarian function and sperm production. Foods rich in folic acid are leafy greens, broccoli, Brussels sprouts, nuts and seeds, asparagus and sprouts.

Pantothenic Acid (B$_5$) supports adrenal function in forming steroid hormones, provides pituitary support, may help male impotence and improves sexual stamina. Foods rich in pantothenic acid are the cruciferous vegetables, molasses, fish, nuts and seeds, poultry, whole grains, eggs, and organ meats.

Vitamin C is important for sperm production and motility, and against impotence. Foods rich in Vitamin C are acerola cherries, strawberries, tomatoes, mangos, avocados and kiwi.

Bioflavonoids support capillary blood flow, are important to healthy mucous membrane tissue and have estrogenic qualities. Foods rich in bioflavonoids include blueberries, cherries, turmeric, ginger, alfalfa, and the white parts of citrus skins.

Vitamin E is an antioxidant important for sperm production that has been used to treat male infertility. Foods rich in Vitamin E are soybeans, leeks, cabbage, wheat germ, nuts, seeds, sprouts, eggs, fish roe, cheese, sardines, and liver.

Lecithin is an important constituent of both vaginal and seminal fluids. Lecithin also affects the sex center of the brain, the transmission of nerve messages for sexuality, and the endocrine glands. Lecithin supplements come from high phosphatide soy or egg products.

Minerals are important for sexual vitality:

I mentioned **Zinc** earlier as a key component of tradition-ally sexy foods. While most of its publicity has been for male reproductive health, zinc is important to the sex lives of both men and women. Zinc is essential in both seminal and vaginal fluids. Its deficiency in men can cause low sperm count, loss of sexual interest or impotence and can contribute to prostatitis. Lack of zinc in women can result in reduced vaginal lubrica-tion. Foods rich in zinc are eggs, whole grains, nuts and seeds (especially pumpkin seeds), organ meats, oysters, and fish roe.

Phosphorus is essential to brain and nerve activity, and along with calcium and magnesium helps maintain sexual desire. Lecithin is the richest source of phosphorus. Foods rich in phosphorus are egg yolks, codfish roe, and seafood.

Magnesium may help the male sex drive. Men rely on magnesium for *testosterone production*, and to overcome pros-tate problems and sterility. Along with calcium, magnesium helps keep you un-stressed. Magnesium rich foods include leafy green vegetables, cornmeal, nuts and seeds, wheat germ, whole grains, seafood and sea vegetables, legumes, and milk.

Calcium may help impotence. Calcium helps your body maintain the right acid/alkaline balance for proper menstrual cycle and female fertility, and vital to the endocrine glands ability to produce sex hormones. Calcium rich food are raw dairy foods, yogurt, nuts and seeds, whole grains, green leafy veg-etables, lentils, rice, onions, parsnips, eggs, and fish.

Potassium affects sexuality through its effect on nerve and muscle activity and by contributing to the right acid/alkaline balance. (See calcium.) Potassium rich foods include blackstrap molasses, soybeans, dried fruits, bananas, nuts and seeds, rice, wheat bran and germ, parsley, lentils, spinach, and avocados.

Iodine is critical to healthy thyroid activity. An underactive thyroid can result in sterility, loss of sex drive, menstrual problems, depression and weight gain. Food sources for iodine are seafood, sea vegetables and pineapple.

Selenium works with vitamin E to promote fertility and helps keep us looking young. Foods rich in selenium are the bran or germ of grains, broccoli, onions, tomatoes and fish.

We've touched on some of the basics of sexuality. A good diet, exercise, and herbs are important lifestyle cornerstones on which to build sexual vitality. We'll talk about them in detail later in this book. But the "heart" of sexual desire is that men and women are different. These differences dramatically affect sexual libido.

Men break down tissue; they expend energy, as in the discharge during sex. They need denser foods, more concentrated proteins, and three times the volume of complex carbohydrates as women.

A man's sex drive and function is largely dependent upon testosterone, sensory stimulation and a good blood supply to the erectile tissues, factors that rely on adequate nutrition.

Diet and exercise are the main pillars of health for men, but the quality of both are woefully deficient in the modern American man's life. Poor farming methods and chemicalized foods have made us one of the earth's most nutritionally deficient nations. Yet for optimal sexual function, men need optimal nutrition.

Most men have no idea how closely regular exercise is linked the their sexual performance. In one new study, 78 healthy, but sedentary men were studied during nine months of regular exercise. The men exercised for 60 minutes a day, three days a week. Every man in the study reported significantly enhanced sexuality, including increased frequency, performance and satisfaction. Rising sexuality was even correlated with the degree of fitness improvement. The more physical fitness the men were able to attain, the better their sex life.

Here are some lifestyle dangers for male sexuality:
1) Long recreational drug use inhibits sperm production.
2) Long heavy metal or radiation exposure damages sperm and chromosome structure.
3) Sexually transmitted diseases scar the vas deferens, obstructing sperm delivery to the penis. If they spread to the testes, infertility results.
4) Smoking does more than damage your lungs. The cadmium contained in cigarette papers interferes with the utilization and absorption of zinc the most important nutrient for male sexual function.

Women build up tissue; they receive energy, then convert and enrich it to create life. They need less protein, for instance, than men, and a smaller volume of complex carbohydrates for conception and fertility.

For women, it all comes down to hormones - those incredibly important, potent substances that seem to be at the root of most women's problems. Hormones are secreted into the bloodstream by the glands, and carried throughout the body to stimulate specific functions. They are the basis for all metabolic activity. Some have almost immediate effects, some have a delayed reaction. But, even in the tiniest amounts, they have, as any woman can tell you, dramatic effects. Even a minute imbalance in ratio or deficiency can cause extreme body malfunction.

Nutrition is also a key for female sexual function, especially as a woman approaches menopause when estrogen levels change. Post-menopausal women should increase their consumption of soy foods and plant hormone-rich herbs, because the phyto-estrogens in these plants produce a mild estrogenic effect in humans. In a recent test, women who consumed the equivalent of one cup of cooked soybeans daily demonstrated distinct signs of estrogenic activity compared to women who did not. The women eating the soy foods also showed an increase in the number of cells lining the vaginal walls, offsetting vaginal drying and irritation.

Note: One cup of soybeans provides the amount of estrogen equivalent to one tablet of Premarin, the most commonly prescribed synthetic estrogen. (Synthetic estrogen is associated with the **increased** risk of cancer. Plant hormones from foods and herbs are associated with **reduced** cancer risk.)

Clearly, men and women are polar opposites at the basic, sexual level. I feel we should consider their needs separately to develop the best solutions.

Probably the best place to start is with what turns men and women on. Are there really any aphrodisiacs?

An aphrodisiac (from the Greek goddess of love Aphrodite), is anything that can arouse or increase sexual desire, or improve sexual potency. Often the definition is expanded to include things that relax sexual inhibitions, stimulate the genitals or other erotic body points, conquer impotence and frigidity, and particularly for men, substances that enhance male erections, help prevent premature ejaculations, and produce more semen.

Mankind's search for aphrodisiacs is probably equal to the search for the Fountain of Youth. People have been known to eat anything that even remotely resembles a sex organ (bananas, asparagus, oysters, etc), even eating the actual sex organs of animals in an attempt to boost sexual vigor.

Of all the things mankind has called aphrodisiacs, herbs have the greatest and most enduring reputation. For literally thousands of years, herbs have been associated with love potions. What's behind this reputation? **Can certain herbs really enhance libido and sexual performance? Is there some herbal smoke behind the fires of passion?**

Recent studies are showing that, once again, science is validating herbal tradition. In fact, it turns out that certain herbs may have a great deal of influence on several aspects of sexual response and performance in human beings. In my own experience, working with herbs and men and women for over 25 years, I can frankly say that some herbs have undeniable qualities that can turn a couple's attention to love.

Herbs don't turn men into supermen, or make women love slaves, but herbs can be a good remedy choice when there are sexual function problems. Normal sexual function requires healthy organs, and balanced glands to produce sex hormones. Herbs, as superior body balancers *that combine with your body, and work through the glands*, are uniquely qualified to help us achieve better gland response and overcome body deficiencies for a healthier sex life.

But they can do even more than that. Herbs can also work quite specifically, often quickly to remedy sexual problems and enrich the sexual experience. The greatest benefit of using herbs to enhance sexuality is that they work so individually with the human body. Herbs are the only substances that I know of on earth that can address the physiology of both men and women effectively.

Let me stress that even herbs with an aphrodisiac reputation don't make you go out and waylay a complete stranger for sex. They enhance and enrich sexual feelings and activity, rather than instigating or overwhelming it.

Are there herbal aphrodisiacs that sexual partners can use together for enhancement? In fact, I find the best way to take herbs with aphrodisiac properties is as part of a whole romantic experience - for example, as compounds that both might take before a romantic weekend.

Hormone and glandular secretions are the basic cause of the differences in a man's and a woman's bodies. Glandular functions, where herbal activity is most energetic, are at the deepest level of the body processes. **Here's how herbs work for men and women for sexual enhancement.**

HERBS FOR MEN

Herbs can be a valuable answer for male sexual health, because the most sexually stimulating herbs contain substances that support male gland and nerve systems in a direct way.

1) Herbs increase energy to the male reproductive system. *Panax ginseng* for example, is a proven source of plant testosterone that can help normalize a man's sexual hormone supply.

2) Herbs can be a primary source of absorbable, safe zinc for men to favorably affect potency and sperm production. Zinc is concentrated in semen, thus frequent ejaculation may diminish body zinc stores. (The reputation of oysters as an aphrodisiac, for instance, is based on its zinc content.) Zinc is also essential in the health of the prostate gland, and it revs up testosterone. If a zinc deficiency exists, the body may respond by reducing sexual drive until zinc levels are restored.

3) Herbs are strong enough to specifically benefit the male system without the side effects of drugs, yet they have broad spectrum activity for long term results. They can act quickly, but are also cumulative to build a strong nutritional base.

What herbs should men consider for their sexual enhancement? Some of the best are listed on the next two pages. Bear in mind that a combination of herbs always works better that any one single herb.

* **Yohimbe bark increases libido** by increasing stimulation of the sympathetic nervous system, which then enhances both desire and sexual pleasure, and also results more rapid penile erections. Yohimbe's aphrodisiac effects are attributed to the enlargement of blood vessels in the sex organs and to the increased reflexes in the lower region of the spinal cord. Yohimbe benefits female frigidity too, by simulating blood flow to a woman's genitals. But it seems yohimbe does not effect testosterone levels as once believed. Yohimbe, and yohimbine, (the FDA approved drug made from yohimbe bark to treat of erectile dysfunction), are best used under the supervision of a health practitioner since some people may experience side effects like anxiety, panic attacks, elevated heart rate, dizziness, headaches and skin flushing. A normal dose of yohimbe is 750-1000mg. Avoid if you have high blood pressure, schizophrenia, heart, kidney or liver disorders, or if taking decongestants or diet aids containing phenylpropanolamine. We tried LIQUID FARMACY SUPER STRENGTH YOHIMBE by Country Life.

* **Potency wood,** *(muira pauma)* a powerful aphrodisiac herb from South America, **helps stimulate male libido** and overcomes erectile dysfunction. A recent clinical study in America has validated its safety and effectiveness in improving both these areas. Dr. Jacques Waynber, an authority on sexual function, conducted a study with 262 patients who complained of a lack of sexual desire and the inability to attain or maintain an erection. After two weeks using a daily dose of 1gm to 1.5gm of potency wood extract, 62% of the patients with loss of libido reported dynamic effects and 51% of the patients with erection failures reported benefits.

Kava Kava produces a mild euphoria and can be gently stimulating to the genital area.

Ginkgo Biloba improves the blood flow in small veins and is extremely beneficial in the treatment of erectile dysfunction caused by lack of blood flow to the penis.

Saw Palmetto is a natural steroid source herb with tissue building and gland stimulating properties to tonify and strengthen the male reproductive system. It is a primary herb for male impotence, low libido, tonifying the male reproductive system. and prostate health.

What about ginseng and sexual vigor? Is it really an aphrodisiac?

Men always ask me about the role of ginseng as an aphrodisiac. Ginseng has been used around the world for thousands of years to enrich sexuality and restore normal healthy sexual function. Ginseng has several undeniable qualities that validate its reputation. Because of its reputation, ginseng is the most exhaustively researched herb on earth.

It certainly lives up to its name of "man root." Ginseng contains a plant testosterone, and is the only known herb to stimulate production of testosterone in the body, so it is especially helpful as a restorative and male body tonic. A wild Manchurian variety found in China has a particularly stimulating effect, increasing testosterone production and encouraging a rejuvenation that testosterone injections do not.

As an adaptogenic herb, ginseng helps the body deal with stress, increasing energy levels and decreasing fatigue. Both animals and humans copulate more frequently when given ginseng. It also seems to increase the weight of the seminal vesicles, as well as sperm count and motility which all increase fertility. For men with an ailing prostate gland, ginseng appears to help healing and normalization of function.

I have worked with ginseng for years as a sexual enhancer. Ginseng can be a man's "best friend" for a body that is stressed, or exhausted. It's best effects do not develop instantaneously, but rather build up, as deep level balance and healthy sexual function is restored over time.

While ginseng won't make a man into a superman, many men do use its benefits for quick, on-call energy. Larger doses of four to six capsules daily for one to two months are effective for more intense stimulation.

Our own research and experience with a wide variety of ginseng and ginseng-like plants shows that a combination of these herbs is far more effective than any single ginseng when addressing sexuality. **Here are some of the reasons why:**

* A ginseng compound addresses a broader spectrum of needs, affecting more body systems with regenerative activity.

* A compound acts as an all-over body tonic to deal with stress, rather than just as a "silver bullet."

* Ginseng formulas perform best as long term revitalizers, because they allow your body to use the fatty acids in the different ginsenosides for nourishment and energy. A compound, for instance, can nourish the adrenal glands, providing stamina without exciting the nervous system.

* While continued use of concentrated panax ginseng may not be advisable over a long period of time, one to two capsules of a ginseng **combination** may be taken over many months for long term revitalization.

Here are some ginseng-based products we've tested:
* TRUENERGY by Ethical Nutrients
* MALE GINSIAC™ extract with potency wood by Crystal Star *(fresh American panax ginseng, damiana, ginkgo biloba, potency wood, gotu kola, saw palmetto, fresh ginger and capsicum.)*
* 10 GINSENGS by Rainbow Light
* GINSTING by Futurebiotics (Ginseng with bee pollen)

Are there any herbs that have a reputation as aphrodisiacs for women?

Herbs with aphrodisiac properties for women work differently than those for men. Their activity is rather to nourish and tone the female glands and organs rather than exert drug-like activity. Action is much deeper in the body, slower, gentler and longer lasting, almost like the sexual experience itself.

Ashwagandha is an Ayurvedic herb with ginseng-like activity that works well for women because it is a gentle energizer, less overheating and aggressive than panax ginseng, and well-suited to a woman's needs. It helps increase female sexual energy without overstimulating.

Dong quai restores a woman to hormone harmony. Often called the "female ginseng" because it acts as an adaptogen to maintain a woman's proper deep body balance, the Chinese consider it to be the queen of all female herbs.

Damiana is a mild aphrodisiac and tonic for the central nervous and hormonal systems, and is a specific in compounds to treat frigidity in women.

Ginseng plants help women's sexuality as well as men's. Ginseng helps preserve the health of female organs, especially in cases where natural estrogen is absent, such as following a hysterectomy, and prevents vaginal atrophy. Panax Ginseng has estrogen-like effects on the female reproductive tissues.

For some women, panax ginseng can be over stimulating and may even cause insomnia. A good way to take the herb is two weeks on and one week off.

Siberian ginseng (Eleutherococcus senticosus), helps restore a woman's body balance, both physically and biochemically. It is often considered more suitable for women than panax ginseng because it modulates hormone release. Russian studies over a 15 year period firmly establish Siberian ginseng as a tonic for improving fertility, boosting energy and relieving the irritability of pre-menopause and menopause.

Fifteen to twenty drops under the tongue of eleuthero extract are usually felt in 30 to 45 minutes. Note: Siberian ginseng can be too stimulating for some women, so herbalists recommend taking it for 14 days, then resting for 14 days before repeating.

Kava kava and ginger root increase blood flow to the extremities, including the genital area.

Herbs with phyto-estrogen properties also exhibit a tonic effect on the female sexual system, and improve blood flow to the female organs. Phytohormone-containing herbs nourish and tone the female glandular and organ systems rather than exert a drug-like effect. Plant hormones are useful for decreased sexual function, atrophic vaginitis and hot flashes.

Dong quai is an estrogenic herb that can alleviate hot flashes and vaginal atrophy during menopause. Coumarins, naturally occurring substances in dong quai exert their actions on the uterus, increasing circulation, tonification and relaxation.

Black cohosh, a phytoestrogen-rich herb with hormone-balancing qualities, is used in female gland toning compounds for PMS, menstrual problems and menopausal symptoms. It helps increase natural fertility by regulating hormone production, especially after discontinuing the birth control pill.

Licorice root's phyto-estrogens have a normalizing effect on the body for fluid retention, breast tenderness, abdominal bloating, mood swings and depression. Its action on the adrenal glands helps maintain energy levels.

False unicorn is a uterine tonic for female infertility and frigidity that balances production of estrogen and progesterone.

Chaste tree berry helps normalize a woman's sex drive, stimulating production of progesterone by balancing abnormally high estrogen levels. It helps for depression, headaches, premenstrual acne, breast tenderness, cramps and bloating.

Here are some herbal products which support & enhance female sexual functions:
* 8 TREASURES by Ethical Nutrients
* SEREN SHEN by Ethical Nutrients
* Crystal Star FEM-SUPPORT™ extract (with *ashwagandha, dong quai,, and damiana)*
* Country Life MAXINE'S INTIMA FOR WOMEN
* Yohimbe 500mg capsules for a tingle. (See Men's section pg.43 for contra-indications.)

We've talked about the sexuality differences between men and women. But clearly libido is "turned on" by the sexual chemistry between men and women. It's a together thing.

Even though we usually hear about testosterone in terms of a man's body, it is the hormone that determines sex drive in both men and women. Testosterone supplements can liven up libido for both genders and it has been found that ginseng contains a phytotestosterone, a plant substance similar to testosterone, that seems to stimulate the production of testosterone in humans. It may, in fact, be the reason for ginseng's long-standing aphrodisiac reputation. Ginseng is also a powerful tonic adaptogen that boosts well-being and stamina.

Aged ginseng provides the best, most balanced ginsenosides (some of the most active constituents of ginseng). Some ginsenosides are stimulating and warming to enhance physical performance, some are loosening and cooling to aid in relaxation. RED PANAX GINSENG is the best type for aphrodisiac activity.

Other herbs that may be used for aphrodisiac activity by both men and women:

Damiana is a sexual energizer for both men and women. Damiana is one of the most popular and safest of all plants as a libido restorative. Damiana works by increasing the messages sent throughout the nervous system, thereby making people more sensitive to touch. Try ginseng/damiana caps before a romantic weekend.

Licorice is a traditional enhancer of sexual vigor for both men and women. It contains glycyrrhizin, a bio-chemical substance similar to human hormones, which helps provide the body with the raw steroidal materials necessary to produce its own hormones. Try Crystal Star's GINSENG/LICORICE ELIXIR™ with *fresh American ginseng and licorice rt.*.

Sarsaparilla is an excellent hormone balancing herb for both men and women. It contains the male hormones testosterone, progesterone and cortin which stimulate the action of estrogen in females.

Bee pollen and royal jelly have new European studies reporting that a mixture of bee pollen and royal jelly results in an increase in sexual activity for both men and women. Each of these substances have steroid hormonal elements similar to those secreted by the pituitary.

I highly recommend Alive ROYAL JELLY vials.

Avena sativa (wild and green oats) Recently, the Institute for Advanced Study Of Human Sexuality initiated a study to explore the aphrodisiac effects of wild oats. Twenty men and twenty women were given 300mg of wild oats extract

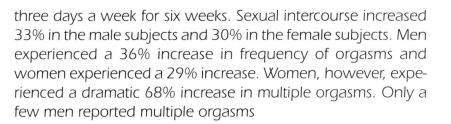
three days a week for six weeks. Sexual intercourse increased 33% in the male subjects and 30% in the female subjects. Men experienced a 36% increase in frequency of orgasms and women experienced a 29% increase. Women, however, experienced a dramatic 68% increase in multiple orgasms. Only a few men reported multiple orgasms

Enhancing the orgasm:

Both men and women experience a 'sexual flush' when sexual activity reaches its peak during orgasm. This orgasmic flush is produced by a release of histamine - a naturally occurring substance in the body.

Anyone who has taken Vit. B_3 or niacin, can attest to the redness and tingling very similar to the orgasmic flush. Niacin also stimulates activity in the mucous membranes of the mouth and vagina to increase sexual lubrication. Some experts recommend taking 100mg of niacin about 30 minutes before sexual activity to enhance the sexual flush, mucous membrane tingling and the intensity of the orgasm.

As an herbalist I find that 1 or 2 cayenne/ginger combination cap produce a more subtle version of the same reaction.

Aphrodisiac products for men and women:
* GREAT DRAGON by Ethical Nutrients.
* Unipro CORDEPHRINE XC by Ethical Nutrients
* Montana Naturals MONTANA BIG SKY LOVING MOOD
* MAXATIVA FOR MEN and WOMEN by Futurebiotics
* OATS, WILD MILKY SEED by Gaia Herbs - an organic fresh plant extract of Avena sativa.
* WILD AMERICAN GINSENG by Hsu's Ginseng Enterprises (woods grown ginseng, more potent than cultivated)
* TRACE-LYTE by Nature's Path. Trace minerals catalyze key enzymes and hormones and are the building blocks for the glands which produce hormones. Trace minerals enhance energy and put a spark into your sex life.

Herbal supplements for male and female sexual vigor.
Here are the most potent formulas I know: Consider taking them for a week before a romantic weekend.

LOVE MALE™ caps by Crystal Star, (with *damiana, guarana, saw palmetto, Siberian ginseng, kava kava, yohimbe, sarsaparilla, muira puama, suma, wild yam, gotu kola, ginger.*)

LOVE FEMALE™ caps by Crystal Star (with *damiana, dong quai, burdock, licorice, guarana, ashwagandha, kola nut, sarsaparilla, gotu kola, parsley, ginger rt.*)

* Crystal Star CUPID'S FLAME™ TEA (with *damiana, prince ginseng, gotu kola, sarsaparilla, saw palmetto, licorice, kava kava, muira pauma wood, angelica, fo ti, ginger, allspice, anise seed.*)

* GINSENG 6 SUPER TEA™ by Crystal Star (with *prince ginseng, kirin ginseng, suma, echinacea ang., pau d'arco, echinacea purpurea, astragalus, St. John's wort, ashwagandha, aralia, Chinese ginseng, reishi mushrooms, Siberian ginseng, tienchi, fennel and ginger.*)

Aromatherapy is one of today's most popular natural therapies. Can it enhance sexuality?
Aromatherapy, a branch of herbal medicine, uses essential plant oils to produce physical and emotional effects through the sense of smell. Most people don't realize that smell is our most rapidly noticed sense. For ancient humans, smell was the body's primary protective sense. Danger could be smelled long before it could be seen. We have all had the experience of "smelling trouble."

Aromatherapy oils have deep subconscious effects on our feelings, triggering memory, lifting emotions and altering attitudes. Essential oils of have been used for thousands of years to enhance the sexual experience and also to lure lovers. The oils act on an emotional, mental and physical level.

Scents are intimately intertwined with our emotions, feelings, and memories. A familiar scent can instantly flood your head with a field of flowers, or paint pictures of your past on the movie screen of your mind.

The fastest way to alter mood state is with smell. The information from scents is directly relayed to the hypothalamus, where motivation, moods and creativity all begin.

The volatile molecules of essential oils work through hormone-like neuro-chemicals to produce their sensations. When the scent of an essential oil enters through the nose, the molecules stimulate a sensory cell that sends a message to the limbic brain where neurochemicals affect the memory and create subtle mood changes. The response from this process can last for hours or days. The reason for this is that the olfactory bulb that directs our sense of smell is part of the limbic system, the section of the brain that controls emotion and triggers memory and **sexual response**.

Scents also influence the endocrine system responsible for hormone levels, metabolism, insulin production, stress levels, body temperature and appetite.

Certain oils can enhance your emotional equilibrium merely by inhaling them. Depending on the oils chosen, they may either calm and relax, or stimulate and energize. Brain-wave studies show scents like lavender increase the alpha brain waves associated with relaxation. Scents like jasmine boost beta waves linked with alertness.

Oils for libido include ylang ylang, patchouli, vanilla, sandalwood and cinnamon.

Sexuality-enhancing aromatherapy oils for men include cinnamon, sandalwood, lavender, patchouli, coriander, jasmine and cardamom.

Oils especially nice for women are ylang ylang, rose, clary sage, neroli and rosewood.

* SENSUALITY by Wyndmere Naturals, (Rosewood, Ylang ylang, Rose Otto, Jasmine)
* SENSUOUS by Wyndmere Naturals, (Palmarosa, Sandalwood, Cinnamon, Jasmine, Rose Otto)
* ROMANCE by Flower Solutions
* APHRODISIAC by Nature's Apothecary.

Can natural healing methods help when men have sexual problems?

Men are most often worried about their ability to achieve and maintain an erection, with the frequency they can have intercourse, and the length of their recovery period after intercourse.

Just to set the record straight, men are capable of retaining their sexual virility well into their 80's. Growing older is not synonymous with inevitable sexual decline. Although the recurrence of impotence increases with age, aging is not a cause of impotence. Even when the amount and force of an ejaculation decreases with age, the capacity for erection is retained.

So, what causes male impotence?

Eighty-five percent of all impotence problems for men are physical, involving circulation or heart problems (the most common cause), drug actions and interactions, sexually transmitted diseases, prostate disorders, nerve diseases like MS, gland and hormone imbalances (sometimes caused by environmental estrogens), alcohol and tobacco. Smoking just two cigarettes a day can inhibit an erection.

Ten percent are psychogenic, relating to stress, performance anxiety or depression.

The small remainder is often due to fatigue, and is usually temporary, once enough rest restores the man's energy.

Atherosclerosis of the penile artery is the primary cause of impotence for almost half the men over the age of 50. Factors that contribute to atherosclerosis are cholesterol and triglyceride levels, high blood pressure, obesity, lack of exercise and smoking) need to be addressed.

Many experts think environmental estrogens may also be part of the problem. We know that they seem to be driving some serious problems for women. The newest studies show they may be adversely affecting the reproductive ability of men, too. Semen analysis tests of both sperm count and sperm quality over the last few decades show us undeniably that total sperm count as well as sperm quality of the general male population has been deteriorating.

In 1940, the average sperm count was 113 million per ml. In 1993 that value had dropped to 65 million. Total amount of semen has also fallen dramatically, from 3.5ml. in 1940 to 2.74ml. in 1993. These changes mean that men have only about 39% of the sperm counts they had in 1940.

This downward trend in sperm levels has led to speculation that environmental, dietary, and lifestyle changes in recent decades may be interfering with a man's ability to manufacture sperm. Although controversial, there is substantial evidence for the devastating role of man-made estrogens.

I recommend that men especially avoid hormone-injected meats and dairy products, and herbicide-sprays to avoid the exogenous estrogen factor.

Products to combat environmental estrogens:
MILK THISTLE Extract: long term support fo the liver.
20 DAY DETOX INSURANCE by Ethical Nutrients
PHYTO-SPROUT PLUS by Healthy Tek, Inc.
LIFE SHIELD by New Chapter

Can diet make a difference in your potency quotient?

In about one quarter of *physiological origin impotence*, lack of normal libido is simply a matter of improving a poor diet. Junk food, saturated fats, high sugars, hard liquor, chemical and processed foods are key factors in a man not feeling "up to it."

I recommend adding mineral-rich foods, such as shellfish, greens and whole grains to your diet, and essential fatty acids, like flax or evening primrose oil - 4 to 6 capsules daily.

■ In particular, add zinc-rich foods to your diet. Zinc is clearly the most important nutrient for male sexual function. Zinc is concentrated in semen, and ejaculation significantly diminishes body zinc stores. Some researchers feel that the body may respond to depleted zinc stores by reducing sexual drive to conserve them. Foods often recommended to enhance male sexual function include liver, oysters, nuts, seeds and legumes, because they are good sources of zinc.

A man's sex drive and function is largely dependent upon testosterone, sensory stimulation and a good blood supply to the erectile tissues, factors that rely on adequate nutrition. **For optimal sexual function men need optimal nutrition**, because their sex drive requires a healthy gland and nervous system. A diet rich in fresh, whole foods is important.

Note: Beyond diet, studies show that exercise is critical at all ages for male sexual performance.

In an incredibly revealing diet and sex study, men with vascular disease were divided into control and experimental groups. The control group received regular medical care and the diet prescribed by the American Heart Association.

The experimental group ate a low-fat, vegetarian diet with plenty of fresh fruits, vegetables, whole grains, and legumes. The men were allowed to eat as many calories as they wished.

No animal products were allowed except egg whites and 8-oz. a day of nonfat milk or yogurt. The diet contained approximately 10% fat, 20% protein, and 70% complex carbohydrates.

The experimental group was also asked to perform stress reduction techniques, like deep breathing, meditation or imagery for an hour each day, and to exercise at least three hours a week. At the end of the year, the subjects in the experimental group showed significant regression of atherosclerosis.

By contrast, subjects in the control group who were being treated with regular medical care and the American Heart Association diet of 30% fat, actually showed progression of their atherosclerosis, and got worse.

A young male body ensures that the penis gets enough oxygen by triggering nocturnal erections - an average of two or three hours worth every night. It's a boy's body recharging his sexual batteries. With each successive decade of life, nighttime erections become less frequent, so it's even more important to have regular waking erections. Tough assignment, I know. But think of it as doctor's orders. Sexual therapists recommend at least three erections a week. There are many avenues for meeting this quota.

Can herbs help a man overcome impotence?
Certain herbs can help. Some herbal combinations can even be applied directly to the abdomen area to help with a better erection. A compound, for instance that has helped men for many years to reduce prostate swelling and inflammation, is also effective in prolonging erections - for both older and younger men.

PRO-EST PROX™ Roll-on by Crystal Star Herbal Nutrition is a product that has been beneficial to many men in this sensitive area. It contains *aloe vera, grape seed oil, extracts of pygeum African bk., wild yam, fresh American ginseng, saw palmetto,*

41

white oak, potency wood, echinacea angustifolia, goldenseal rt., pau d'arco, licorice, burdock, oregon grape rt., European mistletoe, marshmallow, uva ursi, lecithin, ginseng and licorice rt. phytosomes.

Other formulas we have reviewed with good results:
* MASCULEX by Enzymatic Therapy
* ACTION MAX FOR MEN by Country Life.
* MALE PERFORMANCE™ caps, a long term, highly successful compound by Crystal Star (with *saw palmetto, damiana, Siberian ginseng, sarsaparilla, royal jelly, potency wood, gotu kola , wild yam, licorice, dandelion, American ginseng, fo ti rt., yellow dock, capsicum.*)
* LOVING MOOD FOR MEN™ extract, a fast-acting, short term formula by Crystal Star (with *damiana, Siberian ginseng, licorice, wild oats, dandelion, capsicum, yohimbe.*)

We hear a lot about dopamine and sexual impotence. What's the connection?
Certain neurotransmitters, like dopamine in the brain, are like spark plugs to an engine. Dopamine is associated with memory ability, our sense of well-being, and is intimately associated with sexual drive. Dopamine stimulates physiological functions such as strength, movement, coordination, alertness, cognitive functions, mood, and growth hormone secretion. Sexually, dopamine has been found to affect libido, orgasm and ejaculation. Dopamine levels decline in the brain cells as we age, causing sex drive and brain functions to drop, too. A person with extremely low levels of dopamine might develop Parkinson's disease.

Are there any natural substances that increase dopamine levels?
There are three that we know of:
1) **The first is fava beans.** Fava beans have high concen-

trations of L-dopa and are a non-prescription way to take it. In fact, a 16-ounce can offers almost a prescription dose!

2) **The second is Yohimbine.** Yohimbe bark is a source of dopamine and yohimbine. Yohimbine enhances stimulation of the sympathetic nervous system, which releases norepineph-rine, opening the valve to the penis and causing more rapid and frequent penile erections. Even sexually inactive heart transplant patients receiving yohimbe have immediate return of sexual potency in 3 out of 4 cases.

When used alone, yohimbine is successful in over 40 percent of erectile dysfunction cases. But I always recommend that it be used in combination with other complementary herbs, because it may induce anxiety attacks, or aggravate high blood pressure in some individuals. Since yohimbe tends to increase heart rate, those with liver or heart problems or diabetes should avoid its use.

3) The third dopamine stimulator is NADH (**nicoti-namide adenine dinucleotide),** a hydrogen-do-nating coenzyme, a powerful antioxidant. NADH is a metabolite of niacinamide, a form of Vitamin B_3. NADH is available in supplement form.
Note: TYROSINE is an amino acid that **boosts** dopamine levels.

Male Plumbing Problems: your prostate can be your libido's worst enemy.

The little doughnut-shaped gland that lies below a man's bladder can be a source of big problems to many men. Almost 60% of men between the ages of 40 and 60 have BPH (benign prostatic hyperplasia). The prostate's job in life is to secrete a fluid/enzyme mixture for sperm health and motility. As middle age approaches, the prostate often enlarges, strangling the urethra, and causing the early BPH symptoms of frequent urination, trouble starting urination, weak flow and the feeling that the bladder isn't empty afterwards. BPH is not cancer, but an enlarged prostate can eventually completely block the flow of urine, an obviously life-threatening condition. Even if the problem never reaches that state, take care of it immediately. The inability to fully empty the bladder results in a painful bladder condition and dangerous inflammation of the kidneys.

Prostate health is linked to the decline of testosterone production. Enlargement seems to be caused by an enzyme, testosterone reductase, that interacts with testosterone and produces di-hydro-testosterone, a "rogue" hormone form that also affects male pattern baldness. When testosterone is not converted into this metabolite form, the prostate continues its youthful functions and does not enlarge.

BPH responds well to nutritional and herbal support. **Indeed, for many men, natural therapy for prostate problems works better than the most powerful prostate drugs on the market.** When the first signs of increased urinary frequency, reduced urinary flow or prostatic inflammation are felt, consider the following natural therapy program:

1) Take extra zinc - 50 to 75mg daily.

2) Take flax oil - 1 tablespoon added to salad dressing is easy. Or take *evening primrose oil* - 4 to 6 capsules daily.

3) Reduce the cholesterol and saturated fat in your diet.

4) Increase your dietary fiber from fresh produce and whole grains. Men should get about 35 to 45 grams of fiber daily.

5) Take unsprayed bee pollen - 4 TBS. or 10 capsules daily.

6) Take selenium, an antioxidant mineral that attacks free radicals and is essential for sperm production. In combination with vitamin E and zinc, selenium provides *relief from enlarged prostate symptoms.* Sea vegetables are an excellent source of selenium and carotene antioxidants. Two tablespoons of chopped, dried sea vegetables sprinkled over a soup or a salad provide a supplemental amount of these nutrients.

An herbal formula providing these nutrients is Crystal Star's IODINE/POTASSIUM (*with kelp, alfalfa, dandelion, dulse, spirulina, barley grass, nettles, borage sd. and watercress*).

Herbs Can Be Your Prostate's Best Friend

Certain herbal combinations are clearly successful in helping men to avoid surgery or a hospital visit. The two suggested here have broad spectrum antibiotic, astringent, and anti-inflammatory activity. They help reduce prostate enlargement and inflammation of the male urethral region. They contain herbs to overcome stopped or weak urination, and soothing agents to help relieve pain and congestion. Effective improvement has often been evidenced within 48 hours. So reduce your fat intake, boost your fiber intake and consider herbal formulas.

* PROX™ FOR MEN capsules by Crystal Star (*with saw palmetto, pygeum Africanum bk., licorice, gravel rt., juniper, parsley, potency wood, goldenseal, uva ursi, marshmallow, ginger, suma, capsicum and hydrangea rt.*)

* Crystal Star PROX™ FOR MEN extract with Pygeum Africanum, (*saw palmetto, white oak, potency wood bk., echinacea angustifolia, pau d'arco, goldenseal rt., marshmallow, pygeum africanum bk., uva ursi.*)

* PROSTATE CAPS by Solaray.

What about natural and herbal therapy for female sexual problems? While men are worrying about what turns them on, women are more aware of what turns them off!

One of the definite things that turns them off is painful intercourse. During reproductive years, estrogen stimulates the cells lining the vagina to maintain proper moisture. But during menopause, the vaginal lining may become thin and dry due to reduced circulating estrogen. Intercourse may become painful, and some women experience increased susceptibility to vaginal infection. Herbs can often come to the rescue.

For immediate relief, I recommend the topical use of vitamin E oil, or an oral extract of two Chinese herbs for vaginal fluids, Crystal Star's WOMEN'S DRYNESS™ (with *licorice rt. and dendrobium*) to produce more fluid in the membranes. Panax ginseng also helps the body produce fluid. Taking vitamin E internally helps improve blood supply to the vaginal walls.

Drugs, chemicals and synthetic medicines, working as they do outside nature's cycle, often do not bring positive results for women. Clomiphene citrate, for instance, a fertility drug, stimulates the brain to release luteinizing hormone, which causes an egg(s) to mature and be released from the ovary. One of the drawbacks is that more than one egg may be released and this can result in an unwanted multiple pregnancy that is neither fair to the parents nor the future of the children.

Drugs usually try to add something unnatural to the body, or act directly on a specific problem. Herbs as concentrated foods, are identified and used through the body's own enzyme action. They are gentle, but effective nutrients that encourage the body to do its own work, and recover its own balance.

Herbal therapy nourishes in a broad spectrum, like the female essence itself. A woman's body responds to it easily without side effects. We find that most women know their own bodies better than anyone else, and can instinctively pinpoint even deep level areas of imbalance that need support.

Many hormones are protein based, and we now know that proteins from herb and green plant sources can be very effective for human gland and hormone health.

Herbs for women's sexual and reproductive balance:

Dong quai is effective for female problems like infertility, irregular periods, and can tone a weak uterus by promoting metabolism within the organ. It helps PMS, cramps, bloat, hot flashes (especially when taken with evening primrose oil), menopause-induced anxiety and fatigue. It increases hormone uptake by the body, especially helping to balance estrogen levels and is widely used as a hormone regulator to "keep the female system female." Because dong quai may stimulate bleeding, pregnant women or women with fibroids should not take it.

Vitex (Chaste Tree Berry) is prized for its ability to restore balance to the female hormonal system. Vitex stimulates luteinizing hormone (LH) release from the pituitary gland, which in turn, promotes ovulation. Vitex helps create an effect in women that leads to a balancing of the ratio of the hormones estrogen and progesterone by acting on the regulatory hormones in the pituitary gland. This helps relieve symptoms of female hormonal imbalances such as depression, cramps, mood swings, water retention, weight gain, headaches, and breast tenderness. Vitex extracts are also useful for uterine fibroid cysts.

Licorice root helps menstruation problems in women with irregular periods. Licorice also helped with elevated testosterone and low estrogen levels (often occurring in polycystic ovary disease). Its phyto-estrogens (especially estriol) have a normalizing effect on the body for fluid retention, breast tenderness, abdominal bloating, mood swings and depression - very important for balancing female hormones during menopause. Some studies show that licorice has breast cancer inhibiting qualities through its phytohormone constituents.

Wild Yam has hormone-like compounds that support the body's own hormone production. Menstrual cramps, irregular menstruation, hormone-induced headaches, hormone-related acne, PMS and menopause-related irritability have all been soothed by wild yam. The weak hormonal activity of wild yam in the body may help prevent habitual miscarriage due to hormonal insufficiency.

Effective products for women's sexual balance:
* Transitions PROGEST cream as directed.
* Crystal Star PRO-EST BALANCE™ roll-on (with *aloe vera gel, wild yam, fresh American panax ginseng, dong quai, damiana, licorice, black cohosh, sarsaparilla, burdock, peony, oatstraw, raspberry, rosemary, vegetable glycerine, cellulose thickener, grape sd., ginseng and licorice rt. phyto-somes, lecithin and vit. E as a preservative.)*

Sexuality and Aging

It is a myth that people lose their sexuality in their later years, experience declining performance, poor responsiveness and lack of libido. **Aging and sexuality do not go hand in hand if you pursue a natural and healthy life-style.**

Let me tell you a story about sexuality and aging. The people of Vilcabamba, an Andean mountain village in Ecuador are some of the longest-lived people in the world. And they not only live much longer, they also remain more vigorously sexual in old age than any other peoples. In fact, the men and women of Vilcabamba are notorious for their love affairs, and sexual passion is an important part of their lives, regardless of age. Centenarian men even father children. Records show that healthy sperm was taken from one man when he was 119 years old. Some women continue to menstruate until they are nearly 70 years old.

What is their secret?

The Vilcabambans grow and eat whole grains, like maize, barley, millet, rice, rye, and wheat; they eat soybeans and other legumes. They eat a large variety of fresh vegetables regularly which include cabbage, cauliflower, celery, broccoli, tomatoes, squash, zucchini, carrots, and peas. They eat a wide variety of tropical fruits. They eat only about half the protein of Americans, and most of their protein and fats are of vegetable origin. Their diet is notably low in animal fats. Meat is eaten about once a month. The Vilcabambans make cottage cheese and a thin yogurt from goat's milk or (less often) from cow's milk. Eggs are eaten slightly cooked or even raw. They seldom if ever eat anything refined.

But their story has greater depth; there is a deeper secret to the Vilcabambans' long life and prolonged sexuality. The richly fertile soil that feeds their crops and the water that they drink are both exceedingly rich in **trace minerals**!

A new study in the Journal of Applied Nutrition shows that the minerals supplied by the Vilcabambans' country lifestyle contribute to their exceptionally long life and amazing capacity for sexual activity. Vilcabamba village lies in a valley where water washes silt from a mountain behind them. They get a constant supply of trace minerals in a balanced concentration from soils and mineral-rich water rich throughout their lives. Researchers stated that the Vilcabambans maintain their health and longevity from the activation of their cell enzymes by these minerals. Essentially, they are thriving on enzyme therapy!

How is the water and foods that we eat in America so different from the water and foods in the Andean village of Vilcabamba? Years ago, it was easy to receive almost all our essential minerals and trace minerals from fresh vegetables, grains and fruits. Today, many of these once abundant minerals have been leached from our soils due to modern farming techniques. Acid rain, pesticide applications, deforestation, and chemical fertilizers all contribute to our mineral depletion. Even eating organically grown foods isn't the whole answer, because our soils are over-farmed and mineral deficient.

Our drinking water is far from mineral rich. When we drink bottled water in an effort to get pure water, many of its natural minerals have been distilled or "purified" out.

In addition, stress, over-use of drugs, laxatives or antacids, fighting an illness, and toxic environmental chemicals rob or bodies of minerals.

Our body nutrients, like proteins, carbohydrates, fats, sugars, vitamins, enzymes and amino acids, need minerals for activity. Our body processes, like circulation, thought, memory and digestion depend upon the action of minerals, particularly electromagnetic energy.

Dissolved electrolyte minerals in the blood act like spark plugs for the body. Electrolytes dissociate into charged particles, called ions, creating an electrical charge in the body which is necessary for life. The drinking water of Vilcabamba contains highly mineralized, electrically charged water.

The industrialized world can no longer depend on its food and water to supply us with the amount of minerals that our bodies need. (Sometimes I wonder just who is a "third world" country, and who is an "advanced society.")

Getting more minerals may be one of the most important things you can do for your health, longevity and sex life.

Pure Air

Vilcabamban men are extraordinarily potent. Researchers feel that air quality in Vilcabamba - air rich in negatively charged ion particles, was a contributing factor to their sexual longevity. (Most of us have felt invigorated and "charged" when we stand in the wind right before a storm, experiencing an electrical charge of negative ions.)

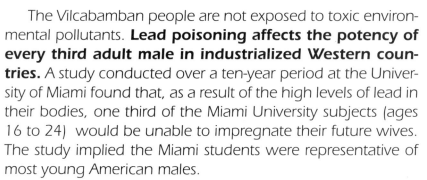

The Vilcabamban people are not exposed to toxic environmental pollutants. **Lead poisoning affects the potency of every third adult male in industrialized Western countries.** A study conducted over a ten-year period at the University of Miami found that, as a result of the high levels of lead in their bodies, one third of the Miami University subjects (ages 16 to 24) would be unable to impregnate their future wives. The study implied the Miami students were representative of most young American males.

Researchers speculated that overexposure to low-level lead in the air from factory pollutants and automobile exhausts (especially lead) significantly lowered the sperm count in these young men. In other words, their fertility fell because of heavy-metal toxicity.

Americans are reacting to heavy-metal toxicity surrounding them by developing impotency, vaginal atrophy, premature ejaculation, frigidity, menstrual difficulties, loss of libido, retrograde ejaculation, infertility, and premature sexual aging. Especially hard hit are those industrial workers regularly exposed to heavy metals such as mercury, nickel, copper, cadmium, arsenic, aluminum, or lead.

Exercise

In the Vilcabamba study, exercise was thought to be a major factor in the long sexuality and general health of the people. Exercise is an integral part of life for the Vilcabambans who have almost no degenerative disease. They walk everywhere, especially up and down the steep hills of their land, and work six days a week farming.

In essence, they are providing themselves with their own built-in form of chelation therapy. Regular vigorous exercise is a natural chelating agent; it cleanses the body of the atherosclerotic plaques that clog the arteries.

In the Western world, free radicals, highly active compounds produced when fat molecules react with oxygen, play a key role in the deterioration of the body. Although free radicals are a part of normal metabolic breakdown, our bodies experience excesses of these cell damagers from chemicalized foods and pollutants throughout our environment. After years of free radical assaults, cells become irreplaceably lost from major organs, like the lungs, liver, kidneys, and brain. This loss is seen as a primary cause of the deterioration effects of aging. When the cells of the nervous system are attacked, for instance, senile dementia or Alzheimer's disease results. Cell damage to connective tissue results in loss of skin tone and elasticity, and to degenerative aging affects, like atherosclerosis and arthritis.

Note: Lowering the fat in your diet is one of the single most beneficial steps you can take to reduce free radical damage. A high fat diet depresses the body's antioxidant response to neutralize free radical attacks, and fatty deposits in the tissues harbor environmental estrogens and pollutants.

The Vilcabamban people show us that **following the most natural, healthy life-style we can manage can bring us a long life and keep our sexual zest intact!**

Here are some steps you can take. To understand aging and sexuality, we need to understand the main causes of aging.
    1) Cell and tissue damage caused by free radicals that aren't neutralized when the body lacks antioxidants. Antioxidants are a key to anti-aging.
    2) Reduced immune response that puts the body at risk for disease-causing stress and environmental toxic reactions.
    3) Enzyme depletion in the body due to lack of enzyme reinforcements from food and supplement choices.

Herbs and superfoods can slow the effects of aging and keep you sexually active.

I believe herbs and superfoods like chlorella, spirulina, barley grass and aloe vera can play a big role in our search for the Fountain of Youth. Herbs and superfoods have youth-extending nutrients with far reaching possibilities as health restoratives, and energy givers while keeping us sexually fit. They have antioxidant properties which prevent body components from destruction by free radicals. They have potent nutritional content that can address both the symptoms and causes of a problem. They are full of food-source vitamins, minerals and powerful plant enzymes that make them easy to absorb. Certain herbs are specifics to help better memory, strong gland activity, smoother skin, stamina, endurance, muscle tone, hormone enhancement, and good organ tone - all part of sexuality.

Herbal therapy is a premier therapy for anti-aging.
* Anti-oxidant herbs quench and neutralize free radicals.
* Adaptogen herbs strengthen immunity.
* Enzyme-rich herbs protect against enzyme depletion.

If you decide to supplement your minerals, I recommend herbal sources, or minerals that are in an electrolyte solution / crystalloid structure. **True electrolytes are in a crystalloid form.** This means that the minerals have been reduced, in a special process, so that their particles are small enough to pass through cell walls. This makes them 100% absorbable and very powerful. Providing the body with electrolyte minerals in a crystalloid form bathes it in a chemistry balancing fluid, enabling it to re-establish homeostasis. By restoring electrolyte balance in the body, energy circuits are switched back on and health and vibrancy is regained. Taking electrolyte minerals can not only put a spark back into your love life, it can also keep your sexual battery charged and going.

* Consider TRACE-LYTE by Nature's Path (A true electrolyte formula).

Many people, especially women, tell me that sex gets better for them as they age. They say they are more relaxed, and feel less at risk for an unwanted pregnancy or a sexually transmitted disease.

For both men and women, sex can be a golden time in the golden years if you stay healthy and active.

My best recommendation is to live as naturally as you can. Especially be conscious of your diet and the water you drink. Try to limit the drugs you take, and surgical procedures that you agree to. Modern medicine is wonderful in many ways, but it is concerned with emergency measures, and keeping you alive, rather than your quality of life.

Conventional, drug-based medicine is grounded in science, and the scientific method breaks things down or takes them apart to understand them. Science tends to see things only in pieces, to see a person only in terms of his or her problem. Often the success of a medical procedure is judged on the accomplishment of the technique, with little regard for the quality of life for the person who actually had to undergo it. I know so many seniors who have had "successful" operations and ended up on lifetime drugs and in diapers.

You are a whole person. The drugs or surgery treatments you take for one problem affect your whole body..... and many drugs and surgical procedures have impotence, incontinence and reduced libido as side effects.

Ask questions about every treatment or drug prescribed for you. Make sure you aren't a senior citizen who is alive but has no life, because of medical health care decisions that have taken away your vitality. Promise yourself that, at the very least, you'll take a little time to learn about natural health care. Consider diet and exercise improvements you can easily make yourself instead of spending your days in a doctor's waiting room and letting health care decisions be made for you.

Fertility and Conception
Are You Trying To Have A Baby?

Preconception planning is important in today's polluted environment. Diet improvement and lifestyle changes can lead to successful conception. Herbal nutrition can help support body deficiencies that deter conception.

In America today, one in six married couples of child-bearing age has trouble conceiving and completing a successful pregnancy. Poor nutrition and stress seem to be at the base of most fertility problems.

For men, the main hindrances are zinc deficiency, too much alcohol, and tobacco.

For women, the prime inhibitors are anxiety, emotional stress, severe anemia, and hormonal imbalance. There is a link between infertility and vitamin C deficiency in both sexes.

Reproductive vitality for both men and women is based in the health of the glands and sex hormones.

There are metabolic differences, too, but estrogens, (female hormones), and androgens, (male hormones) are found in both sexes. Women build up tissue; they receive energy, then convert and enrich it to create life. They need less protein and a smaller volume of complex carbohydrates for conception and fertility. Men break down tissue; they expend energy, as in the discharge during sex. They need denser foods, more concentrated proteins, and three times the volume of complex carbohydrates as women.

However, clinical experience has shown that the sexual vitality of both men and women can be improved by a natural (especially organic foods) diet. Herb and vitamin supplements can help supply the metabolic needs of virility or fertility.

About conception testing:

Before you can use natural methods to help conception, an infertility workup to understand the cause of infertility may be useful. It can allow you to target the problem and address it quicker. A workup usually includes a complete physical, sexual history, semen analysis for the man, a blood hormone evaluation for the woman, and a test showing compatibility of the man's sperm and the woman's vaginal secretions.

A physician can also check the possibility of uterine fibroids, endometriosis, ovarian cysts, infections of the reproductive organs or anemia. Lack of ovulation can be caused by anemia, because a women's body attempts to spare blood loss. Treating the underlying cause of anemia may restore fertility.

Mounting evidence from scientific mind-body studies indicate that when too many stress hormones are created in the women's body over a prolonged period, they can disrupt female reproductive hormone balances. Dr. Alice Domar, director of Harvard Medical School's Mind-Body Program for Infertility, says just destressing infertile women sometimes allows them to regain normal hormone function so they can become pregnant.

If an anatomical examination fails to find the cause of an abnormal sperm count, and environmental factors are ruled out, then nutrition may be the key. General malnutrition or specific nutrient deficiencies can result in weak sperm.

Conception diet for both men and women:

A new study by the Corsello Centers for Nutritional Medicine in New York, has found that many young American women in their 20's and 30's have infertility problems related to hormone imbalances. Most of the women studied have plenty of estrogen but are lacking in progesterone. The researchers felt that environmental hormones from foods full of pesticides and hormone-injected meats are part of the problem.

The director of the centers now recommends a super nutrition diet with an all organic food program, the use of soy milk and tofu instead of cow's milk which can be loaded with environmental estrogens; eggs; two to three servings of vegetables; three servings of fruits; six servings of whole grains; beans, seeds and nuts and a salad dressing recipe with flax oil (rich in essential fatty acids necessary for hormonal balance) Sugars, sweets, stimulants and refined products are to be avoided. What an about-face for the medical community!

I also recommend:
- Avoid fatty, fried foods or reduce them to less than 10 percent of your diet. (This is good for your sex life, too.) Low-fat, fresh organic produce, whole grains, seafoods, hormone-free turkey and chicken provide minerals, protein, fiber and complex carbohydrates to build gland functions, while avoiding fats.
- Avoid all chemical-laced foods, and all meats and dairy foods that may be laced with nitrates or hormones. Residues of the estrogens fed to cattle and poultry can interfere with human hormones. Estrogens from pesticides, plastics and environmental pollutants can also bind to estrogen receptors in both men and women and in so doing can depress fertility.

Beyond this general pre-conception diet, here are some watchwords just for men:
A virility, pre-conception nutrition program for a man usually includes a short cleansing diet, then a variety of zinc-rich foods like hearty root vegetables, low fat seafoods like fish, shellfish and sea vegetables, and other protein rich foods like organ meats, nuts and seeds, sprouts and beans, some daily fruit, a little low-fat dairy, and plenty of whole grains. Unless grossly overweight, a man should not be on a weight loss diet while he is trying to father a child. Studies show that fasting or severe food limitation has a direct impact on the testicles. A

poorly balanced diet also inhibits male hormone formulation and reduces testicle response to hormone secretions. A man may see increased potency and sexual vigor within the first two weeks of diet improvement.

How about a preconception diet for women?

The body does not readily allow conception without adequate nutrition. Nature tries in every way possible to insure the survival and health of a baby. Gland and hormone health is the key to reproductive health. The endocrine system is so primary and so potent that it must receive good nutrition for conception success. Conscious attention needs to be paid **by both prospective parents** to a healthy diet and lifestyle for at least six months before trying to conceive.

A woman uses food more efficiently and does not have so much need for an initial cleansing fast. She often benefits more from lots of salads, greens and lighter foods; less fat, no meats except seafoods, very low sugars, and a smaller volume of whole grains and nuts. A women should normalize her body weight before conception. Overweight women are at higher risk of developing toxemia and high blood pressure during pregnancy. Severely underweight women run the risk of premature birth and low birth weight babies. A woman's fertility rise may take 6 to 18 months after her diet change.

Vitamin and herbal supplements can help both men and women to normalize their gland and hormone systems. The programs in this book have years of successful conceptions and pregnancies behind them.

Certain supplements may increase male sperm count in three to six months. **Here are some effective preconception supplements for men. Use this program from one to six months before conception.**

58

1) **Zinc** - from 50 to 75mg. daily for 1 to 3 months, to improve sperm count and sexual function. Zinc is necessary for healthy testosterone production, and helps protect sperm from pathogenic bacteria. I also recommend 2 handfuls of pumpkin seeds daily as a dietary source of zinc. Pumpkin seeds contain two additional nutrients which support male potency - the plant steroid beta-sitosterol, which binds to human testosterone receptors, and vitamin E.

2) **Vitamin C** - 3000 to 5000mg daily for 3 to 6 months boosts sperm health, especially in heavy smokers.

3) **Vitamin E** - 400-800 IU.

4) **Octacosonal** - an active factor in wheat germ and wheat germ oil, helps improve sperm motility.

5) **Beta-carotene** - 100,000IU; all the carotenes (such as lycopene) are potent anti-oxidants for men.

6) **Arginine or Taurine** - 2-4 grams a day of either amino acid raises sperm counts and sperm motility.

Herbal compounds are premier balancers and normalizers for male reproductive virility.

Herbs can be a valuable answer for men who want to have a family. They can increase energy to the reproductive system, (a major area of male strength and longevity), and thus make the whole body healthier. Herbs are concentrated foods that can help give the male body solid foundation nourishment it needs to reproduce new cells, to improve vitality and to favorably affect potency and sperm production. Herbs are strong enough to specifically benefit the male system without the side effects of drugs, and they have broad spectrum activity for long term results. They can act quickly, and are also cumulative in the system to build a strong nutritional base.

Herbal formulas containing one or more ginseng species can address male needs for reproduction.

Ginsengs and herbs with ginseng-like properties act as male

body tonics to deal with stress and anxiety. As system balancers, they help regenerate and revitalize. Ginseng's benefits can be used as quick, on-call energy, or as a long term nutritional supplement. A ginseng combination may be taken at a dose of one or two daily over several months for strengthening restoration, or in larger doses of four to six daily for one to two months for more intense stimulation.

The following ginseng-rich formula contains absorbable herbal nutrients for energy, endurance and vitality. It nourishes the adrenal glands without caffeine stimulants, and provides vigor and stamina without exciting the nervous system. It is a source of B_{12} for cell development with naturally-occurring amino acids from bee pollen.

* GINSENG SIX™ SUPER ENERGY CAPS by Crystal Star (with *bee pollen, Siberian ginseng, gotu kola, fo ti rt., Chinese kirin ginseng, prince ginseng, suma, aralia, alfalfa and dong quai*)

A ginseng-based energy tonic supports glandular functions and overcomes fatigue. The following formula also contains extractions of sarsaparilla root and saw palmetto berries, both clinically successful in boosting male testosterone production. It includes two powerful ginsengs: suma, or Brazilian ginseng, rich in germanium and allantoin to enhance immune strength; and Siberian ginseng, a nutritive tonic to stimulate circulation.

* SUPER MAN'S ENERGY™ extract by Crystal Star (with *sarsaparilla, saw palmetto, suma, Siberian ginseng, gotu kola, capsicum.*)

Ashwagandha is a great tonic that has the ability to strengthen, tone and regulate. It is used as a primary sex tonic in Ayurvedic medicine, increasing male sexual energy and male sexual problem conditions like impotence, sterility and premature ejaculation. *Studies in India have shown that it actually works to increase the sperm count.*

Siberian ginseng, especially as an extract, has long been known as a superior adaptogen herb for men, increasing energy and healthy blood chemistry balance. It is strengthening to the whole circulatory system, improves mental and physical stamina and boosts sexual energy.

Note: Synergistic results occur when the above combinations are taken with *evening primrose oil* to promote prostaglandin balance.

Men need minerals, trace minerals and amino acids for hormone production and sperm health.
Minerals play a key role in a man's ability to have a child. Low zinc levels, in particular, have been linked to low testosterone levels and decreased sperm production. The best supplementation regimen for fertility seems to be 50-75mg of zinc for three to four months while trying to conceive. Longer than that without a break, or higher dosage than that, interferes with copper absorption, and sometimes impairment of immune function.

Trace minerals like chromium, selenium, manganese, boron, and molybdenum are clearly involved in healthy hormone balance. Taking minerals and trace minerals from a broad spectrum herb-based supplement is a good choice, because assimilation is easy and efficient for your body. Look for a formula like Crystal Star's MINERAL SPECTRUM™ (with *nettles, Irish moss, watercress, alfalfa, yellow dock root, dandelion, barley grass, kelp, parsley, borage seed and dulse.*)

Potassium is the other specific mineral for men trying to conceive. Potassium strengthens the heart and circulation, and combats fatigue. This is especially important for male virility and conception, since potassium controls hypertension, depression and stress. Unfortunately, although potassium sources are abundant in nature, normal potassium food amounts are less; and today's stressful life-styles require more potassium than regular food intake provides. Organically grown herbs, sea vegetables and green grasses provide optimum metabolic activity for potassium nutrient, as in this all-natural potassium-rich plant compound:

    * IODINE/POTASSIUM™ caps by Crystal Star (with *kelp, alfalfa, dandelion, dulse, spirulina, barley grass, nettles, borage sd. and watercress.)*

Amino acids have also proven to be important supplements for men addressing infertility problems. Besides the well-known boost for testosterone, **L-Arginine** supplementation can help increase sperm production and motility. Even men who have not been helped by other treatments have seen significant improvement with a dose of four grams daily.

L-Carnitine supplementation at a dose of 500mg daily, *along with* chromium picolinate 200mcg daily has also shown success for increased sperm count and motility as well as general improvement in circulation and metabolism.

    * Natural amino acid sources, such as **bee pollen, royal jelly and propolis**, working through the body's own processes, can provide an even deeper level of support.

Today's fast pace and changing lifestyles seem to demand that men be Supermen. A man must be strong physically during workouts and sports, supportive emotionally in relationships, balanced under stress, mentally creative and quick, and sexually keen and virile.

While a good diet and exercise are the main pillars of health for men, today's hectic yet sedentary life-style doesn't encourage men to eat fresh foods or allow for exercise unless a conscious effort is made.

It is now known that men are the infertile partner in 40 percent of infertility cases, and a contributor to the problem in another 20 percent in a couple's inability to have a child.

Here are some natural solutions for common male fertility problems:
1) Anatomy problems like enlarged scrotal veins impair sperm formation. *Exercise and/or alternating hot and cold sitzbaths may restore fertility.*

2) Glandular diseases can interfere with the hormonal control of sperm production and therefore fertility. *Saw Palmetto, a specific for prostate problems, is also a superior gland balancer and normalizer.*

3) Infections of the prostate and epididymis (a tubular structure on top of each testis) can interfere with sperm production or block the exit of sperm from the body.
If you don't want to take chemical antibiotics during pre-conception, I recommend an herbal combination with antibiotic properties, like Crystal Star's ANTI-BIO™ capsules or extract (with *echinacea angustifolia and purpurea root, goldenseal root, capsicum, myrrh, yarrow, marshmallow, black walnut, elecampane, and turmeric.*)

Bodywork is important. A man should:
1) Minimize obstruction to his conduction system by avoiding tight bikini underwear and high bike seats.
2) Protect fragile sperm by avoiding long, excessive heat to the genital area. Refrain from hot tubs, saunas, hot water beds and electric blankets while trying to conceive.
3) Alternate hot and cold sitz baths to stimulate circulation to the reproductive area.
4) Get early morning sun on the genitals for 15 minutes daily.

Lifestyle habits are important, too.

* Avoid or reduce consumption of tobacco, caffeine, and alcohol. (Moderate wine is ok until conception.)

* Get light exercise, and morning sunshine every day possible. Many men find that morning sunshine on the genitals helps. It may be a little difficult finding the privacy you need, but men tell me it's worth it.

* Take alternating hot and cold showers to stimulate circulation and glandular secretions throughout the body. Apply alternating hot and cold compresses to the abdomen or scrotum to increase circulation to the reproductive areas.

The diet, drug and career life style choices made by modern women have curtailed her ability to conceive children. Many women have turned to fertility drugs or mechanical fertilization methods to insure pregnancy. Each of these medical or surgical procedures has risks or unpleasant and/or dangerous side effects.

Herbs gently enhance a woman's fertility environment through gland, hormone and prostaglandin balance.

In my experience, herbal remedies are a primary choice for a woman's body to encourage fertility. Herbs are gentle, safe easily absorbable, and contain in a balanced state, the very elements that women need to promote conception.

Herbs are full of absorbable minerals, vitamins and amino acid precursors. An herbal formula for conception might focus on iron and calcium rich herbs, with pantothenic acid and bioflavonoids to enhance the body's ability to form healthy tissue. It should include herbal phytohormones to stimulate the best hormone environment for conception. Such a compound could be taken for 3 to 4 months prior to conception, and might look like this:

* Crystal Star CONCEPTIONS TEA™ (with *dong quai, black cohosh, royal jelly, licorice, sarsaparilla, damiana, wild yam, fo-ti, burdock, yellow dock, scullcap, ginger and bladderwrack.)*
Note: Ashwagandha, the great Ayurveda tonic (especially for sexual energy) is *used to treat female sterility and infertility.* Adding *ashwagandha* extract drops to the tea gives it an extra "fertility boost."

A different kind of herbal compound to improve fertility might act as a female system tonic and toner. It could be taken over the six month period before conception as a balancing agent - a resource for keeping the female body "very female."
* FEMALE HARMONY™ caps *by Crystal Star (with dong quai, damiana, burdock, sarsaparilla, licorice, red raspberry, oatstraw, nettles, dandelion, yellow dock, rosemary, hawthorn, peony, angelica, fennel, rose hips, ashwagandha, ginger, rehmannia, cinnamon, chamomile.)*

Six other herbs that can help restore female fertility:
* **Vitex** (Chaste Tree Berries) is prized for its ability to restore balance to the female hormonal system. Vitex creates an effect in women that helps to stabilize the ratio of estrogen and progesterone by acting on the regulatory hormones in the pituitary gland, and supporting the endocrine system to operate efficiently at a "master" regulatory level. Vitex stimulates luteinizing hormone (LH) release from the pituitary gland, which, in turn, promotes ovulation to normalize periods so that women can plan their conception times more easily.

* **Dong quai** is a ginseng-like herb that promotes female fertility through regulating and tonic actions. It is effective in normalizing irregular periods, and can strengthen and tone organs. It is widely used as a hormone regulator by normalizing estrogen, stimulating estrogen absorption if body levels are low; occupying estrogen receptor sites to block stronger

estrogens if body estrogen levels are high. Dong quai may set off bleeding; you should not take it once you become pregnant or if you have fibroids.

* **Black Cohosh** is a phyto-estrogen herb with hormone-balancing qualities. It increases natural fertility by regulating hormone production.

* **Licorice Root** is used as a uterine tonic for maintaining and/or restoring good hormonal and reproductive health. In one study involving women who could not ovulate, normal ovulation was successfully induced, by utilizing an extract of licorice root.

* **Red clover blossoms,** a good female tonic, are rich in coumestans and isoflavones, estrogen-like compounds that may promote fertility, particularly in estrogen-deficient women.

* **Siberian ginseng** (Eleuthero) is a tonic that can improve fertility by enhancing overall health and vitality. It also acts on the brain to promote regulation of reproductive hormones.

Herbs can help ease obstructions that might be preventing conception.

Fibroids, ovarian or uterine tumors, endometriosis and prolapsed organs often cause inflammation and infection, reducing the ability to become pregnant. An herbal combination with antibiotic, elasticizing and toning activity can allow the body to begin to shrink unnatural tissue overgrowths so that conception may occur. In conjunction with EVENING PRIMROSE OIL, Vitamin E and a low-fat diet, improvement has often been quite rapid.

I have worked with two formulas that address this problem. The first should be used for one to two months.

* WOMAN'S BEST FRIEND™ caps by Crystal Star (with *gold-enseal rt., squaw vine, raspberry, cramp bark, rose hips, dong quai, sarsaparilla, peony, false unicorn, uva ursi, ginger, blessed thistle, rehmannia and lobelia.)*

After inflammation or infection is reduced, a second formula may be used for longer term normalization.

* WOMAN'S BALANCE FIBRO™ caps (with *pau d'arco, burdock, goldenseal, black cohosh, dandelion, yellow dock, ashwagandha, dong quai, ginger, astragalus, licorice and raspberry.)*

Other gland balancing supplements we work with:
* DONG QUAI SUPREME by Gaia Herbs.
* EVERY WOMAN by New Chapter.
* ROYAL JELLY by Y. S. Royal Jelly & Honey Bee Farms.

While we're considering gland and hormone balancing, this technique can help both men and women solve infertility problems.
Poor glandular activity in either the man or woman is a very common cause of infertility. Herbal compounds can provide gentle broad based gland nourishment that may be used by both sexes for better endocrine balance, and proper hormone secretions.

Adrenal gland function may be specifically involved in sexual energy problems. The adrenals are constantly being called on to react to the stress in our lives. As that stress increases, the adrenal glands overwork to various stages of exhaustion, which affects sexual interest and performance. Herbs help stimulate the adrenals by providing nutrient support. An energy rise is often quite noticeable as the adrenals become nourished. Adrenal support herbs provide quickly absorbable nutrients without adding central nervous system stimulants or animal glandular tissue.

An adrenal support compound for men may be taken daily for the six months prior to conception. Best results are achieved when this formula is taken with 2 teasp. of the highest potency royal jelly daily.

   * Crystal Star ADRN ACTIVE™ extract works best for men (with *licorice root, sarsaparilla rt., bladderwrack and Irish moss.*)

   * ADRN-ACTIVE™ caps by Crystal Star work best for women (with *licorice rt., sarsaparilla rt., bladderwrack, uva ursi lf., Irish moss, ginger rt., astragalus rt., capsicum fruit, rose hips vitamin C.*)

   * For general gland balance for both sexes, use Crystal Star's ENDOBAL™ (with *sarsaparilla, Siberian ginseng, Irish moss, licorice, fo-ti, dong quai, black cohosh, gotu kola, saw palmetto alfalfa, kelp, ginger and spirulina extract.*)

Should a woman go on a body cleanse if she is having trouble conceiving?
A natural fertility program for women might easily include a bowel cleansing for one to two weeks to help rid the body of many of the biochemical imbalances caused by food malabsorption. (See HEALTHY HEALING 10th Edition for a good, easy colon cleanse.)

After the cleanse, the best plan is to improve your nutrition to an optimum level to boost poor digestion and intestinal functions that probably aren't working very well due to stress, and the accumulation of toxins.

Helpful bacteria should be added for intestinal ecology: INNER ECOLOGY by Prevail, or KYO-DOPHILUS by Wakunaga (three potent strains).

Supplements for your pre-conception colon cleanse:
- VITEX caps daily.
- New Moon's GINSENG/GINGER WONDER syrup in water as a tea to stimulate the digestive tract and to fight fatigue.
- Two teaspoons of high potency royal jelly and honey daily. (I like Bee Alive's ROYAL JELLY vials). Modern French research shows that royal jelly acts like a natural hormone, and is especially rich in B vitamins to stimulate the female sex glands.
- Folic acid 800mcg 2x daily.
- B complex supplement 75-100mg daily.
- Vitamin C with bioflavonoids - 1000 to 2000mg daily.
- Vitamin E - 400IU twice a day
- EFA's like EVENING PRIMROSE OIL - 2 to 4 capsules daily.
- Antioxidants like SELEN-E with lecithin by Schiff or COENZYME Q$_{10}$ by Arrowroot Standard Direct.

Beyond herbs and vitamin supplements, minerals are key factors in conception readiness for the female body.
While most women know that extra minerals are important during pregnancy for bone and tissue growth, it is not so well known that minerals are also the building blocks of hormone health for reproductive capability. Calcium, iron and silica are fundamental for the development of good body infrastructure and blood composition.

Herbs can supply minerals to overcome deficiencies.
We know that pregnant women need extra calcium and iron. Herbs are especially effective as rich sources of absorbable, balanced minerals and trace minerals. Herbal sources can be the best way to get these minerals if you're pregnant.
- They are taken in by the body's own enzyme system.
- They are rich in other naturally-occurring nutrients that encourage the best uptake and use by the body.
- They provide an optimum-use bonding agent between the body and other foods it is taking in.

- But their main advantage is that they are so gentle and so easy on a woman's rapidly changing body and delicate system balance during pregnancy.

For example, iron supplements constipate a woman during pregnancy; yet she needs extra iron for blood and bone building and to combat anemia and toxemia.

Herb source iron is a good non-constipating choice. It includes inherent vitamins C and E for optimum iron uptake. it also supplies other supporting trace minerals and measurable amounts of calcium and magnesium for increased absorption.

* IRON SOURCE™ caps by Crystal Star (with *beets, yellow dock, dulse, dandelion, borage sd., parsley, rosemary, alfalfa.*)

* or IRON RICH HERBS by Nature's Apothecary

Another example of a hard-to-assimilate, but needed supplement during pregnancy is silica. Organic silica is critical to calcium absorption for the early stages of bone development in a baby, in addition to its well-known involvement in the growth of strong teeth, skin and a healthy circulatory system.

An herbal silica source **is best taken as an extract** in water during pregnancy. The following formula also has synergistic calcium and magnesium.

* SILICA SOURCE™ EXTRACT by Crystal Star (with *horsetail grass, oatstraw, and organic carrot extract.*)

* or COMPLETE SILICA by Trace Minerals Research

Calcium and magnesium molecules are large, and difficult for pregnant women to assimilate from sources like limestone, egg or oyster shell, or even some of the amino acid chelated formulas. A **calcium** compound of herbs naturally includes magnesium for optimum uptake, and most are also rich in naturally-occurring silica to help form healthy tissue and bone.

* CALCIUM SOURCE™ CAPS by Crystal Star (with *water-cress lf., oatstraw, rosemary lf., dandelion rt., alfalfa lf., pau d'arco bk., borage sd., carrot rt. crystals.)*

A broad spectrum herbal mineral combination with the benefits of natural GLA for prostaglandin balance could be taken for three to four months prior to conception. It has all the benefits of easy-to-take minerals in one.

* MINERAL SPECTRUM™ CAPS by Crystal Star (with *parsley lf. & rt., nettles, yellow dock, watercress, alfalfa, Irish moss, barley grass, dandelion rt. & lf., kelp, borage sd. and dulse*).

* or MEZOTRACE sea minerals by Mezotrace Corporation.

Natural iodine therapy shows great promise for female thyroid balancing needs. Many women have corrected infertility problems simply by adding iodine foods to the diet. Pregnant women who have inadequate iodine are more prone to give birth to cretin babies, a form of retardation.

Natural iodine from macrobiotic quality sea greens and herbs is a key factor in the control and prevention of a variety of gland deficiency conditions. Adrenal exhaustion, kidney and liver malfunction are likely to be improved.

Sea vegetables and iodine-rich herbs have superior nutritional content. They transmit the energies of the sea and earth as rich sources of vitamins, minerals, proteins, and complex carbohydrates. Ounce for ounce they are higher in vitamins and minerals than any other food group. They convert inorganic minerals into organic mineral salts that combine with amino acids. The human body can use this combination as an ideal way to get usable nutrients for structural building blocks.

Sea vegetables are almost the only non-animal source of Vitamin B_{12}, necessary for cell growth and nerve function. They

provide alpha and beta carotenes, chlorophyll, enzymes and fiber. Their mineral balance is a naturally chelated combination of potassium, sodium, calcium, phosphorus, magnesium, iron, and trace minerals. It is also a natural tranquilizer for building sound nerve structure.

Sea plants alkalize the body, reduce excess stores of fluid and fat, and help neutralize toxic metals (including radiation) into harmless salts that the body can eliminate. They purify the blood from the effects of the modern diet, allowing for better absorption of nutrients.

In our modern era of processed foods and iodine-poor soils, **sea vegetables, sea foods and specific iodine containing herbs** stand almost alone as potent sources of natural iodine. Iodine is essential to life, since the thyroid gland cannot regulate metabolism without it. Iodine is an important element of alert, rapid brain activity, and a prime deterrent to arterial plaque. Iodine is also a key factor in the control and prevention of gland deficiency conditions that affect conception.

In fact, sea vegetables, combined with some specific herbs can contain all the necessary trace elements for life. Iodine rich foods are a primary deterrent to spinal birth defects.

Crystal Star makes a natural iodine source combination with the prostaglandin-balancing benefits of GLA.

  * IODINE/POTASSIUM™ caps (with *kelp, alfalfa, dandelion lf., & rt., dulse, spirulina, barley grass, nettles, borage sd., and watercress*)

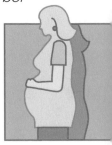

I also recommend taking gentle *kelp* tablets during pregnancy, or using dried sea vegetables in a sprinkle over soups and salads. Just two tablespoons of chopped dried sea vegetables a day is enough to overcome iodine deficiency. Truly remarkable for a single food!

Herbs are gentle and safe for prenatal care.

Herbal nutrition supplements are perfect for the extra growth requirements of pregnancy and childbirth. A developing child's body is very small and delicate. Ideal supplementation should be from food source complexes for best absorbability. Herbs are identified and accepted by the body's enzyme activity as whole food nutrients, lessening the risk of toxemia or overdose, yet providing gentle, quickly absorbed nutrition to both mother and baby.

Herbs for prenatal care are mineral-rich, easily-absorbed and non-constipating. They have been used successfully for centuries to ease hormone imbalances and the discomforts of stretching, bloating, nausea and pain experienced during pregnancy, without impairing the development or health of the baby.

An herbal prenatal support formula can provide a rich source of absorbable minerals and trace minerals necessary for basic body building blocks of bone, muscle and tissue. Some herbs are excellent sources of absorbable calcium and iron, minerals that are easily depleted during pregnancy. (See page 71 for Crystal Star's MINERAL SPECTRUM™ capsule formula.)

Many women, because of morning sickness and general body imbalance, prefer teas as a way to take in nutrients during pregnancy. A traditional, safe red raspberry leaf blend, rich in calcium, iron and other minerals can help strengthen the birth canal, tone the birth canal and uterus against long labor and afterbirth pain, and elasticize the entire area for a quicker return to normal. I have personally worked with many new parents who feel raspberry was a key to their "textbook" births.

* Consider MOTHERING™ TEA by Crystal Star (with red raspberry, alfalfa, nettles, spearmint, lemongrass, fennel, horsetail herb, strawberry, ginger, stevia.)

In fact, many herbs are wonderful during pregnancy
The herbs listed here are good and easy for the mother; good and gentle for the baby. Take them in the mildest way, as hot, relaxing teas, during pregnancy.

* **Red Raspberry Leaf**, as I said, is the quintessential herb for pregnancy. Raspberry is an all around uterine tonic. It is anti-abortive to prevent miscarriage, antiseptic to help prevent infection, astringent to tighten tissue, rich in calcium, magnesium and iron to help prevent cramps and anemia. It is hemostatic to prevent excess bleeding during and after labor, and facilitates birth by stimulating contractions.

* **Nettles** is a mineral-rich, nutritive herb, with vitamin K to guard against excessive bleeding. It improves kidney function; and helps prevent hemorrhoids.

* **Peppermint** may be used after the first trimester to help digestion, soothe the stomach and overcome nausea. It is an over all body tonic and cleanser.

* **Ginger root** is an excellent remedy against morning sickness and stomach cramping.

* **Bilberry** is a strong but gentle astringent, rich in bioflavonoids to fortify vein and capillary support. It is a hematonic for kidney function and a mild diuretic for bloating.

* **Burdock root** is mineral-rich, hormone balancing. Helps prevent water retention in the mother and jaundice in the baby.

* **Yellow Dock root** helps iron assimilation to prevent infant jaundice.

* **Dong Quai** is a blood nourisher, rather than a hormone stimulant. Use in moderation, generally after conception.

* **Echinacea** can help gently stimulate the immune system during pregnancy.

* **Chamomile** is good for relaxation, digestive and bowel problems during pregnancy.

Other herbs for maintaining pregnancy include:
* **Black Cohosh** enhances pituitary secretion of luteinizing hormone with subsequent ovarian stimulation. It contains isoflavone constituents, which are able to bind to estrogen receptors in a woman's body. It is a phytoestrogen, with properties that act as anti-inflammatories, antispasmodics and nervines, qualities that soothe cramping, hormone-related headaches and uterine conditions. Pregnant women should not use black cohosh during the early trimesters, because it can cause premature contractions. Herbalists often use it at the end of pregnancy to stimulate labor, but this should only be done with a trained midwife or health care practitioner.

* **Blue Cohosh** is a uterine tonic that can relax a hypersensitive uterus or increase the muscular tone of a weak uterus. Blue cohosh is also helpful in cases of infertility. Use only during the final weeks of pregnancy.

* **Motherwort** affects the nervous, cardiac and female reproductive systems. It is useful for hormonal imbalances, as a uterine tonic when there is weakness, and cramping.

* **Wild Yam** is a female hormone balancer. It contains subtle hormone-like compounds (the steroidal saponins diosgenin, pregnenolone and botogenin), constituents that support the body's hormone production. The weak hormonal activity of wild yam in the body may help prevent habitual miscarriage due to hormonal insufficiency. WIld yam helps a women through many of the unpleasant effects of pregnancy, like pain, nausea or cramping. It also lessens the chance of miscarriage.

* **Squaw vine** is a fertility and pregnancy strengthener. It is a uterine tonic that can increase uterine tone, reduce uterine congestion and relax uterine spasms.

* **Crampbark and black haw** are uterine sedatives and tonics that have been useful for chronic miscarriage and uterine pain and cramps. These herbs also help condition the uterus for pregnancy and childbirth.

* **False unicorn root** is a uterine tonic and has been used to help women who have a tendency toward pelvic congestion. The herb has been used to help prevent miscarriage and menstrual bleeding due to uterine weakness. **False unicorn, along with black cohosh** (see previous page) **and blue cohosh** should be used for the final weeks of pregnancy only, to ease and/or induce labor.

Certain supplements can also help women to maintain pregnancy:
1) Essential fatty acids (EFAs), from *evening primrose or flax oil* help reduce the risk of toxemia during pregnancy.
2) B Vitamin Complex - helps guard against several types of birth defects, and reduces the risk of toxemia.
3) Folic acid is proven to reduce neural tube defects.
4) Vitamin E - helps insure fertility, and is now thought to be a factor in guarding against habitual miscarriage.

5) Zinc - from 15 to 30mg daily for 3 to 6 months. A necessary mineral for conception; helps prevent spontaneous abortion and birth defects during pregnancy.

Natural supplement compounds we have reviewed:
* COMPLETE PRENATAL SYSTEM by Rainbow Light
* MAXI PRE-NATAL by Country Life.

Important Note: Illness, body imbalance, and regular maintenance supplements during pregnancy need to be treated differently from the usual approach, even if your choices are natural or holistically oriented. The mother's body is very delicately tuned and sensitive at this time, and imbalances can occur easily.

Mega-doses of anything are not good for the baby's system. Dosage of all medication or supplementation should almost universally be less than normal to allow for the infant's tiny systemic capacity.

Two other categories of nutrients should be considered for optimal health during pregnancy.

Body building, whole green drinks from green vegetables, grasses and herbs are full of highly absorbable, potent chlorophyllins, complex carbohydrates, minerals, trace minerals, proteins, and amino acids. They combine the best building, energizing qualities of herbs with the stabilizing, rejuvenating qualities of rice and unsprayed bee pollen, and the oxygen and iodine therapy benefits of land and sea greens. Green drinks are a good way to get super nutrition during pregnancy because they are so quickly absorbed with so little disruption to a woman's delicate system balance.

I have personally worked with a number of green drinks. Here are some drinks that pregnant women approved.
* ENERGY GREEN™ DRINK mix by Crystal Star (with *rice,*

barley sprouts and grass, alfalfa sprouts and lf., bee pollen, acerola, Siberian ginseng rt., sarsaparilla, dandelion, quinoa and oat sprouts, chlorella, spirulina, dulse, gotu kola, hawthorn, licorice, apple pectin, stevia lf.)
    * KYO-GREEN *by Wakunaga.*

Bioflavonoids are necessary for both mother and child.
As an integral part of the natural vitamin C complex, bioflavonoids offer a broad spectrum of healthful activity. Since they often occur naturally with vitamin A and rutin, bioflavonoids are best known for enhancing vein and capillary strength, and for helping to control the bruising and internal bleeding experienced in hemorrhoids and varicose veins. But support goes to even deeper body levels. Bioflavonoids also play a key role in new collagen production, with tightening and toning activity for skin elasticity. They can minimize skin aging and wrinkling, especially because of pregnancy stretching. Bioflavonoid supplements are important in the control of excess fatty deposits because they maintain tissue tone integrity.

Think of bioflavonoids as a "tissue tonic," with herbal and citrus sources as a wonderful way to get them. A good natural bioflavonoid-source compound will also be fiber-rich for regularity - a definite advantage during prenatal care!

    * BIOFLAVONOID FIBER & VIT. C SUPPORT™ DRINK MIX **by** Crystal Star (with *pear fiber, cranberry juice, cranberry crystals, apple fiber, acerola cherry, rosehips, lemon peel, orange peel, hibiscus flwr., ginkgo biloba, hawthorn bry., and buckwheat.)*

Bilberry extract is one of the single richest sources of herbal flavonoids in the botanical world. It is especially helpful for pregnant women suffering from distended veins, hemorrhoids, weak uterine walls, and toxemia. It is gently effective for both mother and child at a time when strong supplementation is inadvisable.

Some herbs should be avoided during pregnancy.

Medicinal herbs should always be used with common sense and care. Especially during pregnancy, some herbs are not appropriate. The following list includes contra-indicated herbs.

x **Aloe Vera** - can be too laxative. However, adding two tablespoons of aloe vera juice from AloeLife (any flavor) to a morning juice or smoothie is a gentle remedy for constipation.

x **Angelica** - emmenagogue causing uterine contractions.

x **Barberry** - too strong a laxative.

x **Buchu** - too strong a diuretic.

x **Buckthorn** - too strong a laxative.

x **Cascara Sagrada** - too strong a laxative; can cause cramping and stomach griping.

x **Coffee** - too strong of a caffeine and heated hydrocarbon source; an irritant to the uterus. In extremely sensitive individuals who take in excessive amounts, may cause miscarriage or premature birth.

x **Comfrey** - alkaloid content (carcinogen) cannot be regulated or controlled for an absolutely safe source.

x **Ephedra, Ma Huang** - too strong antihistamine if used in extract or capsule form. Usually gentle enough as a weak tea to relieve bronchial and chest congestion.

x **Golden Seal** - can cause uterine contractions.

x **Horseradish** - too strong for system delicacy.

x **Juniper** - a too strong, vaso-dilating diuretic.

x **Lovage** - an emmenagogue causing uterine contractions.

x **Male Fern** - too strong a vermifuge.

x **Mandrake** - a mildly irritating, too strong laxative.

x **Mistletoe** - emmenagogue causing uterine contractions.

x **Mugwort and Wormwood** - stimulates uterine contractions; can be toxic in large doses.

x **Pennyroyal** - stimulates oxytocin that can cause abortion. May be used judiciously under professional care in the final weeks of pregnancy.

x **Rhubarb root** - too strong laxative.

x **Rue** - stimulates oxytocin that can cause abortion.

x **Senna** - too strong a laxative.

x **Shepherds Purse** - too astringent. May be used after birth to control post-partum bleeding.

x **Tansy** - an emmenagogue causing uterine contractions.

x **Wild ginger** - emmenagogue causing uterine contractions.

x **Yarrow** - a strong astringent and mild abortifacient.

❖

Sexually Transmitted Diseases
How Do They Affect Fertility and Sexuality?

Sexually transmitted diseases are widespread and increasingly virulent in today's world. They are reaching epidemic proportions in some segments of society. New STD's are increasingly pernicious, and reported cases only represent the tip of the iceberg. It is estimated that one out of every five Americans has a sexually transmitted infection - among the highest in the industrialized world. They are a significant health threat at every level of American life.

Newly recognized STD's, like chlamydia, (the fastest rising STD in the country) venereal warts and cervical dysplasia are growing so fast they are being called new epidemics that can't be ignored. There are 4 million new cases of chlamydia each year. Genital warts is also rising fast, particularly among women.

Most STD's are extremely contagious. Even though precautions may be taken during virulent stages when an STD is recognized, they can still be transmitted during inactive or quiescent stages. Because many people are asymptomatic after they are infected, an STD may be unknowingly spread for years.

Women are in greater danger then men. Anatomically, women are more vulnerable to STD's than men, because a man's infected secretions remain in the woman's vagina after sexual ejaculation. If a woman has an STD, the man's exposure is short, because he ejaculates and withdraws. Women are also less likely than men to seek care, largely because most STD's have no symptoms in women, and current diagnostic tests are notoriously unreliable for women.

Female-controlled prevention technology is not yet on a par with the male condom. Female condoms are still new and extraordinarily clumsy.

Be very careful in your choice of sexual partners and sexual practices. Sexual disease consequences are especially severe for women, because they are frequently irreversible and may be life threatening. They specifically damage the female reproductive area, often producing lingering infections, scarring and adhesions throughout the pelvic region which can prevent conception.

The problem goes even beyond the woman herself. Her sexual responsibility may affect not only her ability to have a child, but through transmitted infection, her children's ability to have a child. Because STD's are extremely contagious, they always affect both partners' ability to conceive, no matter who had the disease first.

Here are the severe complications for women from STD's:
* Infertility
* Potentially fatal tubal pregnancy
* Congenital infections passed to the newborn
* Low birth weight and/or premature birth
* HPV, (venereal warts), is a leading risk factor for cervical dysplasia and cervical cancer
* Increased risk of HIV infection at least three-to five-fold

Symptoms may appear 2 to 3 weeks after sexual contact.
In men, STDs weaken sperm production, damage the testes, scar the vas deferens, reduce sexual vitality and cause a lingering low level infection that affects the entire immune response.

In women, STDs damage the reproductive tract, and produce long term, persistent infections that lead to scarring and adhesions throughout the pelvic region. Scarring of the Fallopian tubes can block the movement of both egg and sperm, causing infertility.

What are the best natural treatments for STD's?

For many years, the only treatment for sexually transmitted diseases was long courses of powerful, but immune-depressing drugs. Today, we are rediscovering the power of herbal remedies and other natural treatments against STD's. A strong arsenal of herbal remedies and supplements can fortify the body against both outbreaks and some of the devastating consequences.

Some STD's respond better to natural treatments than others. Those with acute symptoms may require a short initial course of antibiotic drugs to give the body a stabilizing boost. A doctor who is knowledgable about holistic methods can determine whether antibiotics or other drugs are necessary, or whether natural remedies alone will be effective. Even if conventional medicine is used, adding natural therapies under the supervision of a qualified professional with alternative knowledge can greatly assist healing.

It is obviously of utmost importance to take great care in selecting a safe sex partner. Use latex barriers, and avoid unsafe sex practices like anal or oral sex unless you have certain knowledge that your partner is free of disease. Of equal importance is **keeping your body's natural immunity strong against these infectious diseases.**

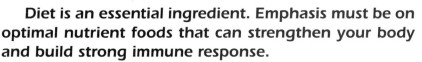

Diet is an essential ingredient. Emphasis must be on optimal nutrient foods that can strengthen your body and build strong immune response.

1) Eat plenty of fresh vegetables, especially high chlorophyll, blood cleansing leafy greens. Have a salad every day with flax oil or olive oil dressing for essential fatty acids.

2) Have a glass of fresh vegetable juice (any blend) daily.

3) Eat only whole foods. No junk or chemicalized foods.

4) Eat about 2 tablespoons of dried sea vegetables daily.

5) Eat yogurt or other cultured foods for friendly flora.

6) Drink pure water, about eight 8-oz. glasses daily.

Here are some supplements and superfoods we work with to help you build immune strength:

* Use enzyme therapy to help break down protein pathogen invaders in your blood supply so they can be destroyed by your immune system. A formula like PUREZYME by Transformation Enzyme Corporation can address infectious viruses, pathogenic bacteria, funguses and parasites.

* Take protective acidophilus, PLANTADOPHILUS by Transformation Enzyme Corporation, or INTESTINAL FLORA FACTORS by Ethical Nutrients, especially if you are taking a long course of antibiotics for an STD.

* Detoxify your liver with MILK THISTLE SEED extract or PURGE FIRE by Ethical Nutrients.

* Take Vitamin C as an antioxidant and antiviral agent to potentiate immune function. I often recommend an ascorbic acid flush as part of a natural healing program against STD's.

* Take antioxidants to neutralize free radicals, balance your body chemistry, strengthen immune response and protect your blood cells from damage. Here are some recommendations:

> MULTI CAROTENE COMPLEX by Rainbow Light
> QUERCETIN 300 by NutriCology.
> LACTOFERRIN by NutriCology - colostrum extract.
> GERMANIUM by NutriCology.

If you have an STD, olive leaf extract may be the natural healer you need.

Olive Leaf Extract, a little known, new supplement in health food stores **is an antimicrobial par excellence.** It has been used with remarkable success against every infective organism type - viral, bacterial, fungal, and protozoan (parasitic) infections. New clinical experience shows that olive leaf extract is an effective treatment for an incredible list of serious modern health problems. Herpes I and II, human herpes virus 6 and 7, HIV virus, flu virus, the common cold, meningitis, Epstein-Barr Virus, encephalitis, shingles, chronic fatigue, hepatitis B, pneumonia, tuberculosis, gonorrhea, malaria, bacteremia, severe diarrhea, blood poisoning, and dental, ear, urinary tract and surgical infections. Recent lab tests have found that olive leaf extract kills 56 pathogens. Amazing!

Olive leaf's powerful punch comes from its **oleuropein**. Oleuropein is a member of the iridoid group, a uniquely structured chemical class. Iridoids are extremely unstable - one member of the iridoid group has the capability to transfer into another group. **This biogenetic characteristic gives the iridoid oleuropein its therapeutic antimicrobial power.**

Microorganisms and fungi mutate into resistant strains in order to survive. The unbridled use of antibiotic drugs for over half a century has helped to breed highly infectious "supergerms" that are drug resistant. Medical researchers are confronting bacteria that have built defenses against the very drugs that once were effective.

Synthetic antibiotics cannot change to maintain their resistance to bacteria. Oleuropeins can change when their environment changes. The chemical structure of oleuropein alters as the microbes mutate. It's a phenomenon that allows oleuropein to continue inhibiting a microbes' growth, spread or survival.

We can see that this has happened over the ages. Ancient olive tree, with oleuropein present throughout all parts of the tree, has protected the olive tree against insect and bacterial predators for several thousand years. Some trees have been alive since before the time of Christ!

Olive leaf extract is rich in natural antioxidants. Olive leaf extract acts as a free radical scavenger, or as a metal ion oral chelator, and inhibits the superoxide-driven reactions.

Olive leaf's oleuropein works efficiently against many harmful organisms in a fashion similar to bioflavonoids.
Here's how:
 ▪ It interferes with certain amino acid processes necessary for the vitality of a specific virus, bacterium or microbe.
 ▪ It inactivates viruses and prevents virus shedding, budding or assembly at the cell membrane.
 ▪ It penetrates into infected host cells and causes irreversible inhibition of microbial replication.
 ▪ It prevents retroviruses from producing enzymes (like reverse transcriptase and protease) that they need to alter the RNA (ribonucleic acid) of a healthy cell.
 ▪ It stimulates the phagocytosis immune system response to pathogens of all types.

Olive leaf extract can have a "die-off" effect. It's a reaction commonly associated with treating an infective yeast syndrome like *candida albicans*. The die-off of infectious organisms caused by an antimicrobial agent like olive leaf can create the sudden release of toxic substances from the dead pathogens dumped into the bloodstream. You may experience temporary allergy-like symptoms or feel unwell for a few days (similar to the headaches or indigestion felt during a detoxification healing crisis).
This is not harmful and is indeed a possible good sign that

olive's antimicrobial agents are working and the infection is dissipating. For preventive purposes, take 250-500mg daily. For treating symptoms, dosage varies with severity.

   * I have worked with and highly recommend PROLIVE Olive Leaf Extract by NutriCology.

Cervical Dysplasia is being called the newest sexually transmitted epidemic by doctors in many countries. Cervical dysplasia is the formation of a precancerous lesion in the cervix. Researchers suspect that two sexually transmitted viruses, Human Papilloma Virus (HPV) and Herpes II are involved, because these viruses also play a role in cervical cancer. Since experts estimate between 40 and 80% of the young, sexually active U.S. population, is infected with either HPV or Herpes II, it is easy to see why cervical lesions are considered especially dangerous.

Does your lifestyle put you at risk for cervical dysplasia?
Do you have multiple sex partners? Have you had multiple partners from an early age? Take a long look at your sex life. Every additional partner increases your odds for an STD.

Do you smoke? Smokers are 3 times more at risk than non-smokers. Avoid smoking, smokeless tobacco and second-hand smoke.

Are you eating a high sugar diet? Do you get a lot of your calories from hard alcoholic drinks ? A sugary diet imbalances your body chemistry to an environment for herpes-type infection. Especially avoid hard alcohol and sugary junk foods.

Do you take oral contraceptives? If you smoke and take oral contraceptives, these drugs potentiate the adverse effects of nicotine, and decrease the levels of key protective nutrients like vitamins C, B_6, B_{12}, folic acid, and zinc. Some oral contraceptives aggravate precancerous lesions like those in cervical dysplasia because of their imbalancing estrogens.

Are you in a sexual relationship with a man who has genital warts or herpes? If you are, you are at extremely high risk of developing a pre-cancerous condition of the cervix. Because the cervix is insensitive to pain, cervical herpes may infect without the woman's knowledge. Use a barrier contraceptive to prevent new contact with HPV or herpes II.

Reconsider your lifestyle. High-risk lifestyle factors must be eliminated for there to be permanent improvement and prevention of further invasive lesions. Most women find their pre-cancerous lesions return after standard surgery alone.
Here is a natural remedy program to help overcome cervical dysplasia lesions.

Improve your diet balance:
* Increase your intake of fresh fruits, vegetables (especially veggies like broccoli and cauliflower), and high fiber foods as protective factors.
* Add folic acid foods like lima beans, whole wheat and brewer's yeast.
* Add vegetable juices and/or green drinks.
* Reduce caffeine, hard liquor and refined foods.
* Add 2 TBS. chopped sea vegetables as a source of carotenes. Add cold water fish like salmon for omega-3 oils.
* Reduce dietary fat, especially from red meat and dairy products. Look for meats or poultry that has not been injected with estrogens or other hormones.

Add neutralizing superfoods:
* Sun CHLORELLA, 2 pkts. daily
* Crystal Star SYSTEMS STRENGTH™ for detoxification
* Solgar EARTH SOURCE GREENS & MORE
* Beehive Botanical ROYAL JELLY with ginseng 2 teasp. daily
* AloeLife ALOE VERA juice twice daily
* Lewis Labs NUTRITIONAL YEAST

Use herbs to jumpstart the healing process.

* Use DETOX™ capsules for one month as a blood cleanser (with *red clover, licorice rt., burdock, vitamin C, pau d'arco, sarsaparilla, alfalfa, kelp, echinacea, garlic, butternut, American ginseng, goldenseal, astragalus, poria mushroom, yellow dock, buckthorn, prickly ash, dandelion, milk thistle sd.*):

followed by FIBER & HERBS COLON CLEANSE™ to rid the colon of re-infection (with *butternut, cascara sagrada, turkey rhubarb, psyllium, fennel, barberry, licorice, ginger, Irish moss, capsicum*).

* Add CALCIUM SOURCE™ to prevent pre-cancerous lesions from becoming cancerous (with *watercress, oatstraw, rosemary, dandelion, alfalfa, pau d'arco, borage, and carrot*).

* Add 2 cups daily of burdock tea, EVENING PRIMROSE oil, 6 daily, and a course of vaginal packs.

Note: Surgery may often be avoided by using botanical vaginal packs, like Nutribiotic GRAPEFRUIT SEED extract, Body Essentials SILICA GEL, or chlorella powder paste, placed against the cervix to draw out toxic waste and slough abnormal cells. Abstain from sexual intercourse during vag pack treatment. (See page 446 of *Healthy Healing* Tenth Edition for detailed instructions on how to make an herbal pack.)

* Alternating hot and cold hydrotherapy or sitz baths will promote immune activity to the pelvic area.

* Crystal Star BIO-VI™ (*usnea barbata*) extract has both antibiotic and anti-viral properties.

* Or consider GOLD LABEL BOTANICAL USNEA & WELL-BEING LYSINE FORMULA by Zand Herbal Formulas.

Note: Women with an advanced stage of cervical dysplasia may have a more natural choice for removing the dysplastic tissue. Some naturopathic physicians today use herbal "surgery," a process where the abnormal cells are "burned" off in a

3 to 5 week process with a twice-weekly application of zinc chloride solution and an herbal *sanguinaria* tincture. The treatments are accompanied by self-applied, nightly herbal and vitamin suppositories. For help in finding naturopaths who performs this treatment (developed by Dr. Tori Hudson) call the American Association of Naturopathic Physicians, 206-298-0125, to obtain a list of practitioners who use this approach.

Anti-oxidants are key factors:
* For 1 month, use an ascorbic acid flush with $^1/_4$ teasp. vitamin C powder every hour until the stool turns soupy. Then take vitamin C 5000mg daily with bioflavonoids for a month.

* Chew Enzymatic Therapy DGL tablets for mouth sores.

* Add B complex with extra folic acid 800mcg 2x during treatment, then once daily to help normalize abnormal cells.

* Add Nutricology germanium 150mg .

Chlamydia, the most harmful of all STDs in terms of infertility for both men and women, strikes an estimated 3 to 5 million people each year. It can afflict any part of the male or female reproductive tract, may be transmitted during either vaginal or anal sex, and bounces back and forth between partners.

* In men, chlamydia causes inflammation of the urethra and testes, watery discharge, pelvic pain and swelling and eventual sterility.

* In women, chlamydia appears as a thick vaginal discharge, affecting the vaginal/vulval area, the fallopian tubes, endometrium and peritoneum. It may also infect the cervix, urethra, eyes, and throat. It scars the Fallopian tubes, causing infertility or ectopic pregnancy, in which the fertilized ovum implants in the tubes rather than the uterus. An ectopic preg-

nancy is very dangerous for the mother's health, even her life because it involves heavy hemorrhaging, great pain, and life-threatening shock if there is a tubal rupture. Even if a uterine pregnancy is achieved, chlamydia increases the risk of miscarriage or premature birth with a high rate of birth defects.

Natural therapy for chlamydia increases circulation to the infected area, cleanses the blood, reduces inflammation and stimulates immunity.

Blood cleansing herbs have had success against chlamydia infection. Treatment should be started as soon as infection is known, and should continue for 1 to 3 months. Look for an herbal compound like Crystal Star DETOX™ caps (with *goldenseal, red clover, licorice root, pau d'arco, echinacea, sarsaparilla, burdock, alfalfa, barberry, panax ginseng, garlic, kelp, milk thistle seed, and dandelion, among others*).

A new Japanese study finds that berberine, an active constituent in goldenseal and barberry motivates macrophages, cellular scavengers that gobble up offending organisms like STD bacteria and viruses in the body.

The above herbal formula may be taken with:
* a daily green drink, and/or 15 *chlorella* tabs daily,
* 6 garlic capsules
* 6 CoQ$_{10}$ 60mg capsules daily,
* beta-carotene 150,000IU
* vitamin C, 5000mg. daily.

Healing fluids with flushing and anti-inflammatory properties should be increased. I recommend cranberry juice, watermelon juice, carrot and cucumber juices to promote urination.

Herpes Simplex Virus 2 (HSV-2) is the most widespread of all STDs, affecting between 50 and 100 million Americans. It is a lifelong infection that alternates between viru-

lent and quiescent stages. It may be transmitted even when there are no symptoms. Transmission is by direct contact with infected fluids from saliva, skin discharges or sexual fluids. Symptoms for both men and women include headache, stiff neck, fever, pain, swelling and itching in the genital area, genitals blisters that swell and become festering ulcers, and shooting pains through the thighs and legs.

Babies can pick up the virus in the birth canal, risking brain damage, blindness, even death. Recurrent outbreaks may be triggered by emotional stress, poor diet, food allergies, menstruation, drugs and alcohol, sunburn, fever, or a minor infection. Men are more susceptible to recurrence than women. Outbreaks are opportunistic in that it takes over when immunity is low and stress is high. Optimizing immune function is of primary importance.

Herpes is serious. It needs healing on all fronts. Most drug treatment offers short-term relief, but threatens long-term health. Educating yourself about natural medicines to deal with serious gynecological conditions gives you a choice.

Diet & Superfood Therapy: Good nutrition is critical against herpes. Body chemistry balance is essential.

* Go on a short three day cleanse (see page 157 of Healthy Healing 10th Edition for details on cleansing diets) to alkalize the body. Have plenty of fruit juices, and a carrot/beet/cucumber juice or potassium broth each day. Take 2 teasp. sesame oil daily. Avoid citrus fruits during healing.

* Then keep your diet consciously alkaline with miso soup, brown rice and vegetables. Add cultured vegetable protein foods such as tofu for friendly G.I. bacteria. Increase consumption of fresh fish (rich in lysine).

* A diet containing significant amounts of arginine aggravates herpes. Foods to avoid include chocolate, nuts, like peanuts, almonds, cashews, walnuts, seeds, like sunflower and

sesame, and coconut. Foods containing a moderate amount of arginine should be eaten with discretion. These include wheat, soy, lentils, oats, corn, rice, barley, tomato, and squash. Avoid these foods until outbreak blisters have disappeared. Immune-suppressants like caffeine, alcohol, and tobacco should also be eliminated from your diet.

  * Reduce dairy intake, especially hard cheeses, and red meat. Eliminate fried foods, nitrate-treated foods, and nightshade plants like tomatoes and egg-plant.

Effective superfoods:
  *Crystal Star ENERGY GREEN™ drink.
  *Nutricology PROGREENS with flax oil.
  *ALOE VERA juice every morning.
  *Green Foods GREEN MAGMA.

Herbal treatment has had remarkable success against herpes, both in remitting symptoms, and reducing outbreaks.

Here's a jump start herbal program:
  * To neutralize toxins, strengthen liver function and cleanse the blood for 3 to 6 months: Crystal Star HRPS™ capsules 4 daily (with *astragalus, yellow dock, l-lysine, echinacea , bupleurum, gentian, red sage, Oregon grape, myrrh, marshmallow, wild yam, sarsaparilla, vitamin E and poria mushroom.*)

  * To reduce inflammation and swelling: Crystal Star ANTI-FLAM™ caps (with *white willow, St. John's wort, echinacea root, white pine, gotu kola, red clover, devil's claw, alfalfa, burdock, dandelion, chamomile, uva ursi, ginger*);
  or quercetin with bromelain caps for almost instant relief.

  * To overcome replication of the virus, Crystal Star ANTI-VI™ extract (with *lomatium dissectum and St. John's wort.*)

Lysine compounds are a key. Here's why:
The herpes virus needs arginine to reproduce. Both amino acids, lysine and arginine look similar to the virus. Lysine therapy fools the virus into thinking it is arginine, and the virus will take lysine, if it is available instead, thus blocking virus development, and keeping it from reactivating.

* Apply lysine cream frequently. Take lysine 500mg capsules 4-6 daily until outbreaks clear.

* Apply Crystal Star LYSINE/LICORICE GEL™. (with *extracts of licorice rt., myrrh, and 800mg lysine, in aloe vera gel.*)

* Dr. Diamond HERPANACINE capsules as directed.

Topical applications can work on lesion outbreaks:
* Open and apply to sores: Crystal Star ANTI-BIO™ caps (with *echinacea angustifolia and purpurea, goldenseal, capsicum, myrrh, marshmallow, yarrow, propolis, black walnut hulls, turmeric, elecampane.*) Also take orally.

* AloeLife SKIN GEL or aloe vera gel/goldenseal solution - an anti-viral to soothe and dry out sores.

* Lemon balm extract, cream or oil applied directly.

* St. John's wort oil.

* Premier LITHIUM, 5mg (capsules may also be opened, mixed with water and applied.)

* Enzymatic Therapy HERPILYN ointment.

* Crystal Star ANTI-BIO™ gel, (with *una de gato bk., pau d'arco bk., calendula and propolis*).

Potentiate immune response with antioxidants like:
* Nutricology ALIVE & WELL. (See Olive extract, page 84.)

* Ascorbate vitamin C or Ester C powder $1/_4$ teasp. every hour in water up to 10,000mg or to bowel tolerance daily during an attack.

* Beta carotene or emulsified Vitamin A 50,000IU daily, with Vit. E 400IU 3x daily. Also apply vitamin E oil directly to reduce pain, and shorten the healing time of herpes lesions.

Lifestyle Support Therapy
* Apply ice packs to lesions for pain and inflammation relief. Ice may also be applied as a preventive measure when the sufferer feels a flare-up coming on.
* Get some early morning sunlight on the sores every day for healing Vitamin D.
* Stress reduction techniques like biofeedback, meditation and imagery help prevent outbreaks.
* Acupuncture is effective for herpes.

There's a new natural immunomodulatory, antiviral agent for herpes virus.

Dumontiaceae, a red marine algae can actively affect several herpes types (HSV-I, HSV-II, EBV and Zoster). It works successfully topically as well as internally. Current research on Dumontiaceae has exhibited promising results in controlling and reducing both Herpes Simplex Virus outbreaks.

Red algae affects herpes virus in three ways:
1) Inhibits DNA and RNA formation of the virus

2) It works as a selective immune stimulant which prevents the proliferation of suppressor T-cells, thus allowing the immune system to control the recurrence of herpes episodes.

3) It alters the biochemistry of the body (creating an alkaline condition) that causes an unsuitable environment for the herpes virus to proliferate, *and* allows the body to rebuild healthy tissue.

Note: Immune disorders like herpes cause a body mineral deficiency - Red Marine Algae is a superfood, rich in minerals that the body can utilize easily.

Venereal Warts (HPV) is the most contagious STD, but the symptoms are often latent or unknown by the infected party. Since the incubation period is three to four months for the HPV virus, it can be spread before the carrier is even aware that they have it. Almost 98% of infected individuals have no visible warts at all, even during the most contagious period.

Warts are most often passed during sexual intercourse with an infected partner, but can be picked up from objects that have been recently exposed to HPV and not properly cleaned, such as medical equipment or tanning salon beds.

Men contract venereal warts in the genital and anal areas. HPV in women infects the ovaries, Fallopian tubes, cervix, uterus and vagina, causing painful, bloody sores in the genital area. There is a chronic, heavy, pus-filled yeast infection, painful intercourse and high fever which can lead to brain damage. Even more worrying, HPV causes changes in the cervical cells and is now linked to cervical cancer. HPV outbreaks can be triggered by co-factors, like smoking, herpes, other STD's, or long courses of birth control pills. If you think you have contracted venereal warts, get tested. An annual Pap smear is the most effective screening tool for detecting them in women.

Herbal treatment for venereal warts focuses on a two-pronged attack - topical applications and oral anti-virals.
Here is an effective herbal program:

1) CRYSTAL STAR ANTI-VI™ to overcome replication of the virus, (with *lomatium, St. John's wort and bupleurum*).

Note: Add folic acid 800mcg daily to help normalize cells.

2) Use Crystal Star LYSINE/LICORICE™ gel, topically applied (with *L-lysine, licorice root, aloe and myrrh*)

3) Crystal Star FIRST AID™, an overheating formula to slightly raise virus-killing body temperature during acute stages, (*bayberry, rose hips, ginger, white pine, white willow, capsicum*).
Note: Overheating therapy in general is effective for reducing warts. See page 178 in Healthy Healing 10th Edition by Linda Page for technique.

4) *Golden seal/chaparral* vaginal suppositories (powders mixed with vitamin A oil) have been extremely helpful for women with venereal warts, rendering many disease-free.

5) Aloe vera gel application along with 2 glasses of aloe vera juice daily; or steep several garlic cloves in a 4-oz. glass of aloe vera juice and apply 2x daily.

6) Matrix GENESIS H_2O_2 OXY-SPRAY daily for a month; then rest for a month, and resume if necessary. If noticeable improvement occurs in this first month, returning to this treatment may not be necessary. The body's defense forces will have taken over and can better continue on their own.

Many men and women are opting for safe, effective natural medicines for STD's. Whether you choose conventional medicine, alternative healing avenues, or combine both in a complementary process, the real prescription for healing is knowledge.

❁